Piercing The Veil
Revealing Illusion with God's Reality

David Carlson

Copyright © 2016 David Carlson

All rights reserved.

ISBN : 978-1-329-85454-3

DEDICATION

This book is dedicated to the *crowd of witnesses* that came before me which lead to my salvation and encourage me, my daughters, my family and the Body of Christ, our church.

ACKNOWLEDGMENTS

There are so many people to thank on this journey we call life and the part they have played in the discovery of who I am in Christ. My parents are just the beginning as they came from a perspective of faith learned through their parents. My brothers that encouraged my spirit of adventure and helped rein me in when the ride got a little rough. My dear daughters enabled me to put into perspective a father's love and to see Christ.
Thank you.

I also recognize the value of being part of something so much bigger than myself as a member in the Body of Christ. I thank my early church and bible Camp Ojibway which built a foundation for me to come back to and the Ministry of Minnesota Adult and Teen Challenge which pointed to God as a means to recovery. Pastor Anthony Bass of Endurance Church, *Live well, finish strong* you are a true servant leader. I love the men that make up my Saturday morning bible Study and the encouragement I get from doing life with kingdom builders, *prayed up and battle ready*. Pastor Dave and Mark, putting on the full armor of God with you, is a blessing. Adam, my brother from another mother – God put us in the same current to sink or swim; we saved each other – *keep on swimming, keep on swimming*.
Thank you!

FORWARD

I was excited when I discovered that David Carlson was writing a book. If you don't know David, then you have to trust me when I tell you that he has the disposition of a "skilled adventurer on a mission." He is a leader with a solid grasp on godly wisdom. He is capable of accomplishing anything he sets his mind to do. Thus, when he answered the call to help his contemporaries find freedom from the monolithic deception in which they are currently submerged, by contrasting that deception with the truth of God's Word and personal experience, I knew that he would be successful.

"Piercing the Veil" reminds me of a man on a riverbank yelling at the top of his voice, "Danger!" Yet, those whom he intends on saving have to choose to either trust this stranger's voice or allow themselves to be carried along by the current. "Piercing the Veil" not only conveys the fact that conventional wisdom has subtly conditioned us to accept our current Western values as common sense and objective, which is wrong, but he challenges us to move past discovering God's reality to embracing our God-given mission for our lives.

Intellectual, articulate, daring, engaging, humorous and prophetic describe the tone, tenor and theme of "Piercing the Veil." It's an authoritative message of perception, redemption and restoration. This clarion call is a timely work that has the latent capacity to stir the soul and inspire the people of God to stand up for God even if they are standing alone!

Read this book, and share it with those you care about.

Pastor Anthony Bass

INTRODUCTION

God created us for so much more than we accept as our lot in life, or even strive for. You are invited to go on a journey that will change your life as the illusion of what we accept as real is exposed with the reality of God's truth. We chase the world standard of performance-driven success, measured with numbers on a balance sheet, valued by commas to the left of a decimal point.

We live in a time of information overload and misinformation upload, too easily distracted from what really matters. There is a spiritual battle for our hearts; how we spend eternity, hangs in the balance. We are infinite beings in a finite body; the truth doesn't change whether you believe it or not. The truth simply is the truth.

The following pages reveal the illusions we've grown accustomed to believe as true. God created us for great things—to experience life in abundance and to glorify Him where our obedience is a form of worship.

Are you satisfied to settle for less than what God intended for you?

If you want more out of life, pursue God. Seek first the kingdom of God and His righteousness and things of this world lose their luster. I'm not talking about minimalism, or denying all of the wonderful things God has in store for us to experience. Far from that; life in abundance is a different kind of freedom. It's living for more than a paycheck, where giving and loving is more rewarding than hording and stockpiling things of temporal value.

The enemy intends to distract us with glitter and gold where we sacrifice eternity for a moment in time.

Our biggest risk is marginalizing the choice of life and death. Too many people are deceived into believing that being "good" is good enough, or they can earn their wings with good works. We can't do anything to have God love us any more or less than He does. He wants us to choose to obey Him.

Take the challenge, seek God. Don't believe He's real? Ask Him to reveal Himself. Don't believe in prayer? Pray anyway, see what happens.

There are moments in time that define us, critical choices that impact our future from that instant forward and change the trajectory and direction of our existence.

Accept the challenge to allow God's truth to expose the illusions and deception of the enemy that seeks only to steal and to kill and to destroy. Don't allow yourself to be taken out of a pivotal role in your eternity.

Choose life; seek Christ, listen for His voice, follow His teachings and go and make a difference in the world around you.

WHY ARE YOU AFRAID?

In Christian circles, we talk about taking a leap of faith to begin our journey of salvation. I like to think of it more like jumping out of a perfectly good airplane. Once you make the jump, the descent begins immediately; acceleration starts instantly and does not stop until you reach terminal velocity of 120 mph, where acceleration stops and your body is resting on a cushion of air.

We've all heard stories of people rising to the occasion and doing amazing things with a little adrenalin rush. The man who somehow lifts a car to free somebody trapped beneath it at the scene of an accident moments before there is an explosion.

Adrenaline is a unique chemical that enhances the body's ability to perform. Imagine that you are about to board a small airplane with the intent to skydive for the first time. You've signed all the waivers and insurance binders, taken the ground school classes, practiced landing and role-play scenarios. You've been instructed on what to do in case of emergency and understand how the equipment works. You have suited up for the jump and checked your equipment.

As you near the plane, you hear the engine running and feel the wind from the propeller. The door is open and you climb aboard. It's a small plane; there are no seats behind the pilot's chairs, and you sit on the cold metal floor. The plane begins to taxi into position on the runway and gets clearance for take-off.

It slowly begins to pick up speed as it rolls and bounces down the runway, faster and faster. It tips and bounces a little bit. The plane begins its accent; as you feel it leave the ground, there is that instant where speed turns to flight, and you are in the air.

You can feel the plane searching for wind and lift as you climb higher and higher into the air. It takes a while to climb to your jumping altitude, and your anticipation is building. As the plane climbs, you feel your heart race and your breath quicken. You can see the ground fall away, and your depth perception changes to where things begin to lose size.

You have reached your jumping altitude and you hear your instructor say, "Are you ready to skydive?" The answer is "yes," but you can hardly speak it as the door opens. As you move into position, the sound of the wind rushing by is deafening. You fight the wind like a child sticking his hand out the window of a moving car as you reach for a handle bar on the wing of the plane.

You maneuver onto the wing, and fight to maintain grip as the wind tries to blow you away while you move into position. Then it is time.

You must surrender your grip to the fall for it would be more dangerous to go back. One, two, three … you surrender your grip and gravity takes over.

You are falling, picking up speed as you drop from the plane, fighting for some control of your descent. You arch your back and spread your arms and legs, struggling for balance. At some point, you reach terminal velocity, where your acceleration stops, and you are resting on a cushion of air. This is free fall.

Adrenaline is pumping and reaching areas of your brain that only few have experienced. Adrenaline continues to pump throughout your free fall. You pull the ripcord, and the chute opens to control your descent. You have a fully deployed canopy and can enjoy the rest of the exhilarating ride until you are safely returned to the ground.

For days following this experience, your senses are heightened. You have acute vision, enhanced memory, calmness and the ability for decisive, critical decision-making.

Much like being in freefall, living in God's will allows the Holy Spirit to work in you like adrenaline works in the skydiver. Once you've experienced it, you wouldn't want it any other way.

Much like being in freefall, living in God's will allows the Holy Spirit to work in you like adrenaline works in the skydiver. Once you've experienced it, you wouldn't want it any other way.

Did you know?

The other day I was having Subway sandwiches with my teenage daughters. If you ever think you're still cool as a dad and have your pulse on the next generation, think again. Out of the blue, mid-bite of her ham and cheese sandwich, my daughter asks, "Dad, have you seen how animals eat?"

I was caught off guard a little bit and just said, "What?"

"Have you seen how animals eat?" she repeated.

"Well, yeah, honey. What kind of animals? I've seen lots of animals eat."

Immediately laughter broke out across the table from both girls. I was expecting that a Heimlich procedure might be required because they were both laughing so hard with food in their mouths. I didn't know what was so funny, but we were all laughing. They were laughing like I had just said the funniest thing in the world. I was laughing at the girls because they were busting up so bad, and I didn't know why.

"What's so funny?" I could hardly even get the words out of my mouth.

People around us must have wondered if we took some happy pills or something. Once the laughter died down enough, she puffed her chest out, lowered her voice and in her best dad impersonation said, "Well, honey, what kind of animals? I've seen lots of animals eat."

They both started laughing uncontrollably again.

She explained that she was referring to a YouTube video titled "How Animals Eat." I guess it became popular at school and all her friends were watching it between classes on cell phones. Clearly evidence of how technology is helping to enhance our educational endeavors. She pulled it up on her phone and had me watch it.

The video is actually pretty funny. It's a simple video from two college guys goofing around in what could be their dorm room or one of their basements. One of them is in a proper sitting position at a table eating a piece of cake. The video involves the second assailant eating a dessert cake as various animals.

In one case, he wildly comes into view with his outstretched arms slapping his hands together in a scissorlike motion, destroying the cake. The video prompts "Alligator" and moves on to another cut where he hops into view with his elbows tucked up into his body with small arms. He reaches out for the dessert cake and shoves it into his pants while the video prompts "Kangaroo."

These are just a couple of examples from the video; we laughed again as we watched the video, and I realized why they thought I was so clueless.

Later in the day I was thinking how out of touch I was with my daughters. Recalling the lunch laugh, I tried to look at things from their perspective. How could I not have known she was thinking about a YouTube video? All her friends would have known what she was talking about. No wonder my question of clarity was met with so much laughter. I thought to myself, *wouldn't it be nice to be able to know her thought process and understand her perspective?*

So often little grievances and disputes begin as simple misunderstandings and escalate as each individual involved advocate why their perspective is the right one. At the end of the day, the interaction could be viewed by somebody else as just a funny episode where each party misunderstood each other.

We are fortunate as Christians because our Heavenly Father knows us, loves us, understands our perspective and has given us access 24/7/365 through Jesus Christ. He offers the best call support in the business. There are no complicated voicemail prompts to navigate. There is no hold music, and there is no language barrier to work through for help.

Not only does He understand our perspective and predicament, He knows what is best for us. That is where our faith, trust, belief and hope come in.

The better we know Him, the easier it is for us to have hope and believe He will deliver us through our situation. We learn to trust His response and through the process strengthen our faith. It's the *richest cycle* opposed to a *viscous cycle*. To experience the *richest cycle*, we have to start the faith motor.

Are you afraid?

"Born to be Wild," a song made popular by Steppenwolf in 1969 might not sound like the best song to use for a faith analogy, but I think it fits perfectly. The song begins, "Get your motor running, head out on the highway, looking for adventure, in whatever comes our way …."

We serve an awesome God, our lives are an adventure, and He is with us in whatever comes our way. Our faith has to start somewhere, so why not think of it like a combustion engine.

Anybody with even a basic understanding of cars and mechanics knows there are differences between 2 cycle, 4 cycle, horsepower, torque, etc. Not all motors perform the same and not all motors are designed for the same performance expectation. There is a difference between drag racing, NASCAR, and the Baja 1000, but the basic mechanics are similar with compression, a spark, and ignition to get the motor running.

The question becomes, What kind of race are you in for?

As Christians, we need to take care of our hearts much the same way a mechanic and driver takes care of a car's motor. We've got to pay attention to what fuels our heart so it runs as designed. The wrong fuel mixture will cause the motor to build up gunk and cause mechanical failure.

Our gunk comes at us from a lot of places in a lot of different ways. It comes from the people we hang around with, our physical intake, what we eat and drink. It comes from what we do with our body in the form of exercise and activities or lack thereof. What we watch, what we read, what we listen to. Our gunk comes from every direction, in every form, all of the time.

As a Christian, God is with us. The Holy Spirit resides in us and Jesus walks with us 24/7/365, and we've been painted with a target from the evil one. Our target is on us 24/7/365: "the thief's purpose is to steal and kill and destroy" (John 10:10). Our world is a battlefield, and we are in a spiritual war. The evil one is like a sniper out there looking to take us out. "Be alert and of sober mind. Your enemy the devil prowls around like a roaring lion looking for someone to devour" (1 Peter 5:8). But, "Be strong and courageous! Do not be afraid or discouraged. For the LORD your God is with you wherever you go" (Joshua 1:9).

The Bible—God's Word—repeatedly encourages us not to be afraid. He is with us. With God nothing is impossible. Fear no evil, etc. So why are so many books written about fear-based conditions: overcoming fear, fear of failure, intimacy, spiders, and phobias of being afraid. We have built industries around dealing with fear issues.

So why are we so afraid? In a nut shell, the world is full of gunk and running way out of specification on its design parameters. God's design was for perfect communion with Him. His creation included everything for the world to be in perfect harmony with Him. Our free will was and still is a critical component of the original design.

We were supposed to choose to glorify Him in all we do, but we chose sin instead and have been separated from His design from the very beginning. We've been building up gunk ever since.

We serve an awesome God, our lives are an adventure, and He is with us in whatever comes our way

REVEALING ILLUSION

So if you think your life is
complete confusion
because your neighbors
got it made,
just remember that
it's a Grand illusion
and deep inside
we're all the same.
We're all the same...
[Source: azlyrics.com, Styx – "The Grand Illusion"]

Satan's greatest illusion is that he makes sin seem okay, fun, exciting, inviting, even rewarding. Humanity fell short of God's design when sin became part of our historical human experience. Eve accepted Satan's temptation in the Garden of Eden, and we've been operating outside of God's design specifications ever since.

God hasn't left us or abandoned us. He gave us free will, so we could decide for ourselves. We can follow His teachings and the example of Jesus' life or fall prey to Satan's deception; it's that simple.

I picture the scene from "Knight and Day" with Tom Cruise and Cameron Diaz when they are in the car. He is trying to explain the severity of her predicament and the limitations of her life expectancy. He raises his hand setting the mark high and asks, "With me?" then lowers it, "Without me?" Repeating the motion as his hand rises and falls, "With me?, without me?, with me?, without me?" You have to choose.

Most of the friends I grew up with came from a modest, suburban *Minnesota nice* background and shared a common belief that people are basically good. We believed people generally knew right from wrong and good from bad. My friends listened to their parents and for the most part we did what was expected of us. Most of them went to church, at least occasionally. At a minimum, they had heard the message of the Gospels somewhere along the way from somebody, even if it was somebody disputing it. At the very least, they had heard something about God and Jesus.

My childhood experience could be similar or very different from yours. Each of us has our own, uniquely different childhood experience. I've heard many stories from young adults recalling their childhood without happy memories like my youth. They came from broken homes, felt rejected, abandoned, unloved, abused and unwanted.

They would argue that there couldn't be a loving God that would allow things like that to happen: *If God is going to treat me that way, who needs Him anyway?* was their response. There is no need for that type of God. People act one way on Sunday, then do all the wrong stuff and call themselves Christians.

One girl I know was sexually abused by a Sunday school teacher and hated God for that. In a nut-shell, destroying our perception of a loving God is Satan's ploy.

We are not defective; we've been deceived, all of us. It's the illusion Satan has successfully implemented on humanity through all of history. We've got God's original design mixed up, inverted, all backwards. Where God should be first, we have exalted Satan. We were designed to glorify God and have chosen rather to deny His existence or minimize His relativity.

Now you might think, *No I haven't. I'm no devil worshiper. I don't go to séances or make burnt offerings or animal sacrifices or anything like that.*

Most of us don't knowingly worship false gods or make sacrifices. Some do, but most are simply deceived into not realizing they are worshiping idols.

I found this reference to Pagan worship simply looking for some family fun on the weekend.

"Pagan Pride is a free fall event, open to the public that offers education about Paganism to the larger community. In keeping with Pagan Pride International's guidelines, Twin Cities Pagan Pride has offered a fall event since 1998 that includes a ritual focusing on the harvest, a food and charity drive, along with other rituals, discussions, vendors, and entertainment (tcpaginpride.org).

We are not defective, we've been deceived

We have to remember that Satan is skillful at deception, a master illusionist and smooth manipulator. His mission is to steal, kill and destroy. He steals our dreams through many different means. It could be our family and friends discouraging you along the way saying things like, "You can't do … (this or that), people like us can't afford college, and you are too small, too big, too this, too that …" At the end of the day, we settle for our lot in life.

Before we know it, we're unhappy, drink too much, do drugs, fill ourselves full of false abundances and materialism. Maybe you cheat on your spouse, envy your neighbor's stuff so you steal it. Next thing you know, you lost your identity. Your family is gone, you find yourself in jail and somehow it's all God's fault.

This progression has been referred to as a psychological decent into hell and has been written about through the ages: "Divine Comedy" by Dante Alighieri and "Dante's Inferno, Descent into Hell" by Carl Jung, and "Apocalypse Now" by Francis Ford Coppola.

Let's take a closer look. Let's acknowledge that there is light and dark, right and wrong, good and bad, and God and Satan. "Anyone who isn't with me opposes me, and anyone who isn't working with me is actually working against me" (Matthew 12:30).

So if you are not with God and His design, then you are opposed and with Satan's illusion. Satan's illusion starts with him as the center of the universe; the earth is his playground. This might be hard for many so-so, churchgoing Christians to swallow.

They say things like, "I believe in God, I go to church, I pay my tithe, I try to live an honest life, I've never been to jail, I'm not a child molester, I don't really drink that much, I'm not a drug addict." Or as the Pharisee prayed in the temple, "God, I thank you that I am not like other people—robbers, evildoers, adulterers—or even like this tax collector" (Luke 18:11).

With comments like these, we are Pharisees: "At least I'm not that guy ... Look what He's done ... I'm not anything like that ... I'm not that bad ...." When it's judgment day and you say, "I'm not that guy," God says, "Then I will tell them plainly, 'I never knew you. Away from me, you evildoers!'" (Matthew 7:23).

Growing up accustomed to Satan's illusion, people are capable of living a seemingly fulfilled life oblivious to the fact they deny Christ and are preparing a path to Hell. In Satan's illusion, the rules apply to everyone else. We think something like this, *I want what I want, when I want it, and I will do whatever is necessary to get it.*

Initially, it's easy to think this mentality applies only to criminals, gang members and drug addicts. That is why we have laws to govern people without a moral compass, right?

Imagine for a minute that you are one of the bad guys.

You've been running and gunning on the streets and most would say that you fell in with the wrong crowd. However, your perspective says, *Screw them and their rules; I'm a survivor.* Your tough attitude and rough action has earned you credibility with your people. You are the go-to guy and know how to get things done.

People listen to you and do what you say, or they get hurt along the way and wish they had listened. You are results driven and capable of making things happen regardless of what it takes to get what it takes done. You make your own rules and are a man of action. If somebody crosses you, likely they're going to eat a bullet or suffer a severe beating, and you won't give it a second thought or have any remorse.

You like to get your hands dirty and don't mind a little wet work with a knife. You like to watch people bleed, beg, and plead while they gasp for their last breath. Taking a pipe or hammer to a skull is as easy for you as sinking an axe into a wet stump after chopping wood.

Satan's illusion makes perfect sense in the twisted world you live in. You are accepted by your peers. To some you are an inspiration, somebody to look up to and even to be respected.

One day you are showing off your new Mercedes C300 and allow your friend to give it a drive. He's holding a pocket full of cash for you when you stop and run into the store for a pack of smokes and to use the restroom.

While you are taking care of your business, you see somebody pull into the gas station and pull up alongside your car. A guy jumps out of the car with a .44 magnum revolver and shoots your friend in the head through your new car's opened sunroof and then peels out. All you can think about is getting the money out of your friend's pocket and getting away before the cops get there.

Does this sound too far-fetched? Things like this happen every day. Visit a few jails and listen to some stories of what happened and how people got there. Of course, nobody is guilty of anything; there is no guilt in Satan's world.

You can say to yourself, "Okay, fine, there are good people and bad people; I can see how Satan's illusion applies to bad people." You can stick your head in the sand to feel exempt, but the reality is that we judge people all the time. It's easy to say they are bad people, and this doesn't apply to me.

Remember Jesus' story about the plank in your own eye? "You hypocrite, first take the plank out of your own eye, and then you will see clearly to remove the speck from your brother's eye" (Matthew 7:5).

We have a myopic, self-centered perspective and can't see the forest through the trees or keep our eyes off someone else's bobber. What about the sales guy that pads his expense account, or the athlete who uses performance enhancing steroids and the student who cheats on a test or copies a classmate's homework?

Sin comes at us in a lot of ways. We like to minimize our wrongdoing and justify our behavior. In some cases, we've lowered the bar so many times that we need to dig to get under it.

If you don't know God, choose to disregard His word, have lowered the bar so far that you think all is well, then you have fallen subject to Satan's illusion and bought the lie.

If you are not with God, you are against Him. If you are against God, you are on the side of Satan. Satan plays on a global scale and the world is his playground. He is the master manipulator and deceiver, skilled at mixed messages, smoke and mirrors, deception and illusion. He can present something as a skill or even as a gift from God and use it for worldly pleasure against our inner spirit.

His only mission is to steal, to kill and to destroy

BROKEN WORLD

Both sides are fightin'
You don't know who to choose
You're stuck in the middle
And you can't lose
Both sides are talkin'
You've finally seen the light
You'll get it together
But not tonight
[Source: azlyrics.com, Loverboy –
"Queen of the Broken Hearts"]

In the illusion of Satan's deception, the worldview guides your desires. Look at what we idolize, glamorize, and romanticize. The world and our culture define what is beautiful and what success looks like: what to drive, where to live, clothes, jewelry, shoes, and on and on it goes. We get caught up in brand equity and image versus need and functionality.

You need transportation to get to work to earn money to provide shelter, food and safety for your family. You want a luxury car, lavish homestead, five star dining and personal protection.

Anything that gets between you and God can become an idol. "No one can serve two masters. Either you will hate the one and love the other, or you will be devoted to the one and despise the other. You cannot serve both God and money" (Luke 16:11). There is never enough.

Somebody always has more. You have an apartment when a friend buys their first house. You have a house, and somebody buys a cabin. You get a cabin with a canoe and paddleboat, but your neighbor at the lake has a Donzi and Jet Skis.

You get all the things you want for the lake home, but it takes too long to get to the cabin because of traffic and stupid drivers, so you want a float plane. The summer season is too short, so you want a place on the beach in the winter. You like to ski in the mountains, but the commute up the canyon takes too long, so you want ski-in-out accommodations. See how this goes?

Our obedience and priorities

Satan's world has many options and his temptations are tailor made to suit your unique desires. If cabins, boats, beaches, mountains and skiing don't satisfy your appetite, maybe there is a penthouse in Manhattan and all the Big Apple has to offer that can quench your thirst. There is always travel—exotic, remote, historical, classic, artistic—too numerous even to get to in a lifetime. There are wonders of the world: parks, canyons, oceans, rivers, waterfalls, lakes, ponds and pools.

You might say all these things have been created by God for our enjoyment and pleasure, which is exactly true. These things were created for our fulfillment from a loving God that we might live to our potential and glorify His honor, not feel entitled to everything around us simply because He gave us life.

All these things have potential to become our idols, which is where Satan's deception reigns. God wants us to worship Him alone. He provided Himself in Body, Mind and Spirit, and we were created in His image.

So let's revisit the garden. Adam walked with God in the cool of the day. We were created to have fellowship with God, intimate fellowship. We see God around us and often lose perspective that His presence was designed to be tangible around us and evident through how we interact with the world around us. The lie we believe to be true is that God's effectiveness in our world is coincidence, explainable by science, and of our own technological advances.

We don't have to look very far to see the world is broken; we broke it. We've become so separated from God's design from that original fall into sin that we accept chaos and destruction as normal. In the garden, we had everything we needed in perfect harmony with God's design. Then evil entered the picture, and our free will was challenged with our call to obedience. There is nothing wrong with evil to exist around us, but it was never designed to become part of our DNA.

God wants us to worship Him alone

The grand illusion was that God was holding something pack from us. "Don't eat from the tree of knowledge of good and evil" wasn't intended to restrict us; it was to protect us. There was a critical moment, an instant where everything would change and define us. As soon as Eve was presented with confronting the lie of all lies, there was an opportunity to choose. Now she didn't realize the gravity of the decision that hung in the balance: the lies minimized the significant impact of the moment. She was caught up in the allure of something more, something different and something new.

She was deceived into thinking her choice in the moment was insignificant, it's okay: *Surely you will not die.* It's like saying to yourself, *Go ahead, nobody will know, nobody will get hurt. You deserve a break today,* right?

We believe the lie and accept that the grass is always greener on the other side. The impact of the decision in the moment is minimized to allow compromise that cannot be undone.

This narrative fits the profile of every affair ending in divorce and accidental overdose. It fits every infraction of every single person every single time they get behind the wheel and drive under the influence of alcohol or a mood-altering substance.

Now we can add being distracted with technology to the compromise; the bottom line is that decisions matter. As seemingly inconsequential as it may seem in the moment, choosing to look at your incoming text message while driving could kill somebody. That is the truth.

We compromise and rationalize the truth to fit what we want because somehow we believe that we deserve it. Eve believed that she should be able to taste from the forbidden fruit because she wanted to. Her choices—obey or disobey; that is the question?

Much like the question of life itself prince Hamlet debates in the famous soliloquy classic of the 1750 Shakespeare play "Hamlet" - Act 3 scene 1:

> To be, or not to be, that is the question—
> Whether 'tis Nobler in the mind to suffer
> The Slings and Arrows of outrageous Fortune,
> Or to take Arms against a Sea of troubles,
> And by opposing, end them? To die, to sleep—
> No more; and by a sleep, to say we end
> The Heart-ache, and the thousand Natural shocks
> That Flesh is heir to? 'Tis a consummation
> Devoutly to be wished. To die, to sleep,
> To sleep, perchance to Dream; Aye, there's the rub,
> …

"Aye, there's the rub …." I love it. Put simply is it better to obey than to risk death itself for the experience or pleasure? Well, Eve was the pivotal person in that decision, which affects each of us to this day. She chose, in the moment to disobey and serve her fleshly desires. We've been in bondage ever since.

BODY IN BONDAGE

My body tells me no
But I won't quit
Cause I want more
Cause I want more
My body tells me no
But I won't quit.
[Source: azlyrics.com, Young the Giant" – "My Body"]

In Satan's illusion, my body becomes an idol. The world defines what we should look like. The fitness market, which includes health clubs and related equipment, weight loss, cosmetic surgery and enhancing steroids is a multi-billion dollar industry. We pay athletes millions of dollars to represent products they don't even use to endorse products.

Don't misunderstand me: "Do you not know that your bodies are temples of the Holy Spirit, who is in you, whom you have received from God? You are not your own; you were bought at a price. Therefore honor God with your bodies" (1 Corinthians 6:18-20).

There is nothing wrong with taking care of our bodies; we don't but we should. After all, they are God's temple.

When our bodies become an idol, we become our own gods and begin to serve our own flesh. Take a quick gut check: How much time and money do you spend on your appearance versus communing with God? Think about it ... the reality is that most "good people," church going, lukewarm, milk-toast, one-step-in, politically correct Christians really don't spend much time working on their relationship with God.

We might go to church more than a few times a year, be involved in a Bible study and look good on Sunday, but are we really working on our relationship with God?

How would you feel as a parent who devotedly and unconditionally loves your children, when they spend as little time with you as they have to in order to get what they want? They only call you when they are in trouble or need something. They bargain and negotiate with you to bail them out of something they knowingly did wrong that catches up with them. They never call just to talk or to check in with you; it's always about asking for something. They forget about you on your birthday, buy gifts for everybody else and call it Christmas.

> *They forget about you on your birthday, buy gifts for everybody else and call it Christmas*

Does this sound like your prayer life or a healthy relationship with God?

The lure of the flesh

When we serve our bodies and fleshly desires according to the world's perspective based on Satan's illusion, it's easy to become distracted. The body wants what the body wants … right now! Our society is based on quick service, fast food, just in time delivery, instant messaging and instant gratification. Nobody really needs to know anything, because we have all our answers literally at our fingertips. Don't believe me? Try to call somebody you talk to frequently using somebody else's phone; we don't even remember our family's phone numbers anymore.

We don't think about what we are putting in our bodies. Look at what people are smoking or using to get high. There is a pervasive and progressive problem with addiction to alcohol and drugs: drinking, smoking, huffing, puffing, popping, banging, inhaling, ingesting, injecting, shooting, and every other way people can get anything from organically grown tobacco to battery acid into their body.

Satan is deadly serious. It's fun for him to watch us self destruct. He'll even give you the first sip, hit, drag, bump, pull, taste, toke for free. If it doesn't kill you the first time, he doesn't really care. He'll wait.

"Be alert and of sober mind. Your enemy the devil prowls around like a roaring lion looking for someone to devour" (1 Peter 5:8). He wants you to come back for another.

Drug addicts and alcoholics have one thing in common: none used the first time knowing it would cost them everything in the long run. The bottom line is that we are not using our mind to determine what is good for the body.

The flesh comes first, and we don't even think about it until it's too late, the damage is done; addicted to sin, we have to.

Remember in Satan's world there is no guilt, no do-over, mulligan or second chance. Every step away from God's design is a step in the direction of Satan's illusion. Our perception is tainted by the distorted view of the world he has successfully sold us, and we just gobble it up.

Have you ever said "What the hell" or worse? "I don't care; let's just do this." YOLO—you only live once.

Serving the body sounds so nice. It feels so good. It's my body, and nobody is going to get hurt; why do you care anyway? The point is this, Satan doesn't care, ever. He is patient, persistent, pervasive and ready to sneak in the smallest unguarded area to establish a foothold that he can turn into a stronghold over time. He's just waiting for a way in.

We normally think of the body as our physical being and it is, but it is also the body of a group of people. God's children are the body of Christ, others are not.

Look at the same thing on a national or global scale. Look at America: "The Land of the Free," "Home of the Brave," "In God We Trust." Really, we do? Do we really trust in God for decision making in any level of government: in our president, in the executive, legislative and judicial branches, in economic decisions, social programs or our foreign policies?

America was initially explored by early settlers seeking freedom from religious persecution. Look at the language of the Constitution, the Articles of Confederation, Bill of Rights and Pledge of Allegiance. In them, we find an intentional action, a declaration and governing rules around *One Nation, Under God. In God We Trust* is printed on all our currency, and God has shown great favor to the land founded on His holy name.

America is a *Cinderella Story* if ever there was one. We can look at American history and the land of opportunity: "Give us your tired, your poor, your huddled masses yearning to breathe free …."

We started from a few good men and women willing to risk all and have grown into a world leader in just a few generations on the timeline of history. However, separation of church and state established to protect the people from tyranny slowly took God out of America. As a result, little by little our national character has suffered by lowering a standard of righteousness disguised as tolerance while yielding to Satan's deception.

our national character has suffered by lowering a standard of righteousness disguised as tolerance while yielding to Satan's deception

There are sensitive political footballs: abortion, same-sex marriage, taking God out of schools, re-writing historical documents of record, etc. Some people go so far as to link these Christian moral compromises to America's economic downward spiral and weakening presence as a nation on the global scale.

Either you are for Him or against Him; so as a people, nation and country we have compromised biblical values, diluted convictions and sacrificed morality to become more popular. We call it being politically correct. Now I'm not saying that anyone is better than anyone else; as Americans, we are equal and have certain inalienable rights. However, there are biblical laws and governing rules where accepting choices that run contrary to God's word are areas where Satan's deception is masked in the illusion of tolerance.

We don't recognize that the world is broken; we broke it. We don't recognize moral decay, but see advances in technology. We pride ourselves on being self-sufficient, independent and capable. We continue to seek more and find less. We attempt to satisfy an insatiable appetite over spending and addiction.

We continue to relax biblical standards and make compromises for tolerance. We feed our flesh without even giving it a second thought.

The global political perspective might seem out of scope for a study on personal transformation and change, but you eat an elephant one bite at a time. The individual standards and compromises we tolerate personally reflect what we are all about and who we follow.

Remember the childhood game Follow the Leader? The game could be fun or scary depending on who was leading. We can be misled as a people, filled with half-truths, spin and outright deceived. We can lie to ourselves, and others can lie to us and we must recognize that we can be deceived.

DECEIVED MIND

But don't be fooled by the radio
The TV or the magazines
They show you photographs
of how your life should be
But they're just someone else's fantasy.
[Source: azlyrics.com, Styx — "The Grand Illusion"]

Our perceptions, through Satan's illusion, deceit, smoke and mirrors become our reality, not the truth. There is a difference between what we believe as real and what is true. For example, look at bullying in our schools, neglect and abuse in our homes. The experiences of the victims are very real, but the real truth is they are victims of a broken world. The truth is, we are beloved children of God, caught up in the crosshairs of a broken world.

To put this into biblical context, we can look at Adam and Eve and original sin. "In the beginning, God created the heavens and the earth" (Genesis 1:1). He goes on to create light, dark, day, night, heaven, earth, land, sea, vegetation, plants, fruit, sun, moon, stars, swarms of living creatures, birds, sea creatures, land creatures and creeping things.

"Then God said, 'Let us make man in our image, in our likeness ….' So God created man in his own image, in the image of God he created him; male and female he created them. Then God said, 'I give you every seed-bearing plant on the face of the earth and every tree that has fruit with seed in it. They will be yours for food. And to all the beasts of the earth and all the birds of the air and all the creatures that move on the ground—everything that has breath of life in it—I give every green plant for food.' And it was so. God saw all that he had made, and it was very good" (Genesis 1:26-31).

Just so we're all on the same page here: God created everything: light, day, night, birds, bees, plants, trees, earth and seas and gave it all to Adam and Eve. God blessed them and said to them, "Be fruitful and increase in number; fill the earth and subdue it. Rule over the fish of the sea and the birds of the air and over every living creature that moves on the ground" (Genesis 1:28).

Now I don't know what you got for your birthday, but it doesn't compete with EVERYTHING! Imagine a giant terrarium; you've painstakingly taken care of every single detail from soil composition, density, water filtration, salinity content, ph balance, air quality and climate control. You've ensured the perfect balance of everything in it and it was very good, perfect! You place caretakers (male and female) into it and tell them it's all theirs; it's all good, enjoy: eat, drink, have fun.

You've given them control over everything in this terrarium. You spend time with them, walk around with them. You let them name things they discover.

One day the girl is doing her own thing, and you're having some guy time. So you're talking to the guy and say something like, "You like this place? It's all good, right? Everything is pretty cool, isn't it? You like the girl, don't you? I see how you look at her. I made you guys especially for each other. She completes you. I see you guys running around, playing in the waterfalls and stuff. It looks like you like the sun and the beach a lot. The food is pretty good too, isn't it? You'll never run out. It's all for you and her to enjoy."

You have a little discussion about the birds and the bees and tell him they can increase in number, to be fruitful and multiply. Then the guy is like, "Okay, now that's what I'm talking about," and the girl is really in charge after that. There's only one rule though: "But from the tree of the knowledge of good and evil you shall not eat, for in the day that you eat from it you shall surely die" (Genesis 2:17).

So the guy wants to make sure he gets this part right. He asks, "This tree, this one right here? I can't/we can't eat from it, but everything else is good … right?"

God answered, "From any tree of the garden you may eat freely" (Genesis 2:16).

"Except that one" he points, "and if we do, I mean I know we aren't supposed to, but just to be clear. If we do eat from that tree, then we will surely die. That's what I heard."

God confirms.

"Okay, good. I'll catch up to you later, my Lord. I've got to go tell the girl about this."

We obviously don't know exactly what happened in the garden, but Adam heard the rule directly from God himself. The Bible doesn't say he told Eve, but it's reasonable to infer that Adam and Eve both knew they were not supposed to eat fruit of the knowledge of good and evil tree. Genesis doesn't go into detail about how long after they were given this rule that Eve found herself in a discussion with the evil one, Satan, in the form of a serpent.

Deception

"Now the serpent [Satan, evil one, our enemy] was more crafty [and continues to be deceitful, conniving, manipulative, an illusionist] than any of the wild animals the Lord God had made" (Genesis 3:1).

Maybe it went a little something like this.

Adam is off on a hike or something, and Eve is putting together a to-do list for when he gets back and the serpent slithers up and says,

"Hey pretty lady. You look nice today. Do you know what that is?"

He points to the forbidden fruit from the tree of knowledge of good and evil with his tail. Eve quickly admonishes,

"Oh that tree, we're not supposed to eat from that one."

"Why not?"

"We'll die; well, that's what God said."

"Did He really say that? Oh come on, it's not like it's going to kill you or anything. Look at it, it's beautiful; it's so pretty," Satan implores.

"That's what I heard ... we'll die if we touch it or eat from it," she says.

"God told you that personally; you are going to die if you eat this fruit?"

The serpent squirms his way up into the tree and picks a piece of the fruit. He slides back over toward her and lifts the fruit up for her with its body.

"I'm touching it, and nothing bad is happening to me. Are you sure you heard Him correctly?"

"Well, He didn't tell me directly; He told Adam and that's what Adam said He said."

"So you never heard it from Him yourself? What if Adam made the whole story up to keep this good fruit all for him? It sure looks good; it smells good too."

"It does look and smell good," she admits. "But we're not supposed to."

"Oh come on, don't be like that little chicken over there that runs away from everything, just one little taste. It's not going to kill you ...."

We all know the outcome: Eve tastes the forbidden fruit and gives Adam some. He eats it as well, just like that. There has to be more to the story; they certainly weren't thinking when they made that decision. God created everything and gave it to them with one simple rule: Don't eat from that one tree.

Remember, they had dominion over all the animals and creepy things. They had authority, they were the rulers. Why would they listen to what the serpent said? Who is the serpent anyway to say anything and question the rules? He wasn't even privy to the conversation in the first place; it was none of his business. Yet he made it his business: "The thief comes to steal, kill, and destroy" (John 10:10).

We can't blame all the sin of the world on the woman—for something that important. Adam was fully complicit. He could have asked God to come with him when he told her about the forbidden fruit, so they could support each other in staying away from it. When she became deceived and ate of it, instead of joining in on the feast, he could have tried to help her, save her.

He could have said something like, "You shouldn't have eaten from that tree. Oh my God come help us. I told you what He said. Oh my God, my God, help us. Eve my love, maybe He'll forgive you and heal you. Let me go find Him. I'll explain that we made a mistake. Maybe I didn't explain things clearly enough or something. Maybe He'll give you a second chance. Oh I hope you don't die."

He thinks to himself, *Well maybe it's not so bad. I'll miss her, but she's the one that made the mistake. Surely He'll make me a new helper that can listen and follow the rules.*

But no ... he's as dumb as a post and joins in. At least Eve questioned herself and acknowledged that she knew she wasn't supposed to eat it, but Adam just took it from her without even thinking and just ate it. Without thinking, without using his mind and decision making capabilities, he satisfied his bodily, fleshly desire and ate the forbidden fruit. So surely they would die.

In that defining moment, a critical choice was made by the pivotal people who would shape the rest of our human experience. Adam and Eve's children never knew what perfect life was like. None of their descendants knew they began with abundant life and gave it away. The truth is that they succumbed to deception from the serpent, and we've been separated from God's original design ever since.

We can modernize the original sin story with the epidemic growth of addictions to drugs and alcohol across the country. Imagine that Adam and Eve are in high school. They have been friends (going out, going steady, pinned) for a while. They have heard all about drugs and alcohol from their parents and from their teachers at school. They have even learned about sin and obedience in Sunday school. They are basically pretty good kids. They have pretty good friends, are involved in school athletics and do pretty well at school.

One day, some friends from school are getting together after a football game and one of them has some _____ (fill in the blank: pills, pot, beer, whatever). We'll call it *forbidden fruit*. So just like that, it's decision time.

They know it's wrong to even think about trying it, but they are curious. There's this new kid who everybody seems to like. He's pretty cool and has a natural charisma. He tells them that he's done it and it's fun. "You'll be okay, I promise. Just try it."

You are nervous, but the opportunity is available right now. Everybody around you seems to be having fun; they've tried it, so you tell yourself it's okay.

TIME-OUT! *I want to shout or somehow show up super naturally in this moment,* **right now**! *The decision you make in this instant impacts everything about your future. Hear my prayers, learn from my lessons, and don't repeat my mistakes. I pray because Satan's ploy is well rehearsed, tried and proven in his delivery. As soon as you tell yourself it's ok, it's already over.*

So they tell themselves it's okay: one try, one taste, one drink. The really scary part is that it probably won't kill you the first time, but it could. Maybe nothing bad happens the first time, and they get away with it without any consequences. The next time it or something similar is available, it is easier to say yes because that standard has already been compromised, the value diminished, the bar lowered.

Kids die every day from drinking and driving, drug overdose or other preventable accidents. Don't think it's true? Tell that to a friend of mine whose little brother drank a little bit and smoked pot once in a while, tried heroine—something he and his buddies swore they would never do. He fell prey to Satan's ploy and died from an overdose his first try.

Satan is real. He is persistent, patient and unrelenting. He may not kill you on the first taste, but he will not back away.

The illusion of fun, everybody does it, nobody is going to get hurt, I'll never tell are all lies from the pit of hell. They are part of Satan's grand illusion to trick the mind into satisfying the body's desire to satisfy the flesh based on what the world has accepted as being good.

Deep down in all of us, regardless of where you come from and how you were raised, there is an inner voice. Some of us don't pay attention to it and have learned how to quiet it through other noise or ignore it. Most of us can't shut it off completely; there always remains an aspect of decency deep within us. That inner voice or second thought we call our conscience is our spirit.

BROKEN SPIRIT

Every night you'll find me
in the only world I own.
It's a crowded place that's filled with people
all alone.
It's a place that I could write a book about.

>When they let you in, you'll find
>there's no way out.
>There you don't get in,
>'cause there's no way out
>There's just no way out.
>No way out when you're in a world
>of broken hearts,
>in a world of broken hearts.

>[Source: azlyrics.com, Elvis Costello –
>"The World of Broken Hearts"]

Most of us go through life without realizing how self-centered we really are. We put ourselves first by serving our fleshly desires without thinking about repercussions or consequences based on a distorted worldly perspective created by Satan's deception. We are oblivious to the reality that when we serve our flesh, we damage our spirit. The ultimate irony we have in American culture is our interest in "Reality Shows" that are not real.

Talk about a reality show, I picture Satan searching for his next victim like a security officer at a casino watching closed circuit video monitors looking for cheaters. Except he is not kicking back in a recliner with a bottle of witches brew watching the battle of good versus evil in the spiritual realm played out on his reality show called Earth. He is intimately involved, conspiring to steal, kill and destroy every single player's dreams, future and relationships. His reality show goes something like this.

People are divinely appointed to play out a purpose driven life starting from a wide array of beginnings. Some are born with a silver spoon in their mouth and others are born hungry. Each player begins with specific talents and a mission. Each player is provided with various opportunities and challenges throughout the game based on their decisions and responses to situational events.

There are opportunities for hard work, quick money, fun, excitement, romance, intimacy, risk and reward, joy and pain, defeat and perseverance. The players are presented opportunity cards and make choices along the way. They must play the cards that they are dealt and the one with the most money, toys and trophies at the end of the game wins.

There are a couple of big problems: The reality show is for Satan's entertainment only, based on deception and illusion, not truth. Remember Satan's mission, objective and goal is to steal, kill and destroy. The period or timeline for his game is finite, with no do-over, mulligan or magic wand. The truth is that our reality lifeline is infinite, whether you believe it or not. The existence of God, heaven and eternity is not predicated on what you believe.

When we live according to Satan's deception and perform to the standards of an illusion, every compromise of virtue we yield is damaging to our spirit. We solidify Satan's position of authority by submission and allow him to build strongholds in our spirit without our awareness.

Many of us think we're okay. Do you really think so? Based on what? You might look good in church when you are there occasionally, know the words to some songs and raise your hands in worship, but do you have a relationship with Christ?

> *The existence of God, heaven and eternity is not predicated on what you believe*

Spiritual demise

One of the great lies is that we don't need anyone. The role of the "Lone Wolf" is always portrayed as being strong, independent, self-assured, confident and ultimately successful. When the truth is the enemy wants only to steal, kill and destroy. One of the oldest tricks in the book is to divide and conquer. It starts with a lie, grows into an agreement, and settles into a cyclical pattern of reinforcement until the lie is accepted as truth. As this pattern of lie, agreement, reinforcement and acceptance develops over time, our inner spirit perpetually weakens.

Francis Chan is pastor of Cornerstone Community Church in Simi Valley, California and also a prominent speaker and author.

He has this great bit he uses to illustrate our focus on time and our own efforts of preparedness. He uses a rope to illustrate time: It's a long rope that runs across the stage and out the building, representing eternity and an everlasting timeline. Then he shows the beginning end of the rope with about an inch-and-a-half wrapped in red tape that represents our life-line. He cleverly weaves a story pointing out milestones: You get a job, get married, work, work, work, save, save, save, build a 401(k) to prepare for this little bit of red-line remaining called retirement ... and then you die.

Then he begins to pull on the rest of the rope, representing eternity. Hand over hand he pulls the rope, feet turn into yards of life-lines, and the rope just keeps coming. There's no end to the rope. I often say we are infinite beings in a finite world. The notion of eternity is a concept beyond our ability to comprehend. It's one of God's mysteries; only God operates outside of time and space. He is the Alpha and Omega, beginning and the end.

I think of a skydiver in the first few moments of freefall when gravity takes over, and the skydiver has no control over her descent. Try as she might, there is nothing she can do to stop the fall.

That's how we are with time; it's a commodity we cannot control, yet we minimize our choices relative to where we spend eternity.

Our ability to minimize, rationalize and compromise leads to the demise of our spirit. Remember that psychological descent into hell? Well, we've made it real—physically, mentally and spiritually by playing in Satan's amusement park. We bought a ticket for the ride and set out to have some fun. We just didn't expect it to literally last forever and progressively get worse through eternity.

The little voice we hear screaming "Enough is enough" is the Holy Spirit

HOLY SPIRITLESS

Own your world
It's in your hands
Own your world
Strive to find the heart.
[Source: azlyrics.com, Hatebreed –
"Own Your World"]

The Holy Spirit comes to us in the form of helper, counselor, healer, reminder, pacifier, encourager, dreamer and motivator, but the quiet whisper is easily drowned out by the roar of Satan's noise. When we're caught up in the daily routine of satisfying our desires of the flesh and chasing the illusion of Satan's deception, we miss out on God's grace altogether. We are so focused on a distorted perception of reality that our awareness of God's presence is virtually non-existent; we certainly don't pay any attention to an inner voice that runs against the flow of our desires.

Think of the sound board in a recording studio with all of the various dials, buttons and slides for ranges, tempos and mixes. You can have a subtle bass track or percussion that is the foundation of the music. As additional tracks of melody, harmony and lyrics blend, you can lose the bass and beat. In something audible, there is a fine line between what music is and what is noise. Now depending on your generation, background and perspective, you can argue what constitutes good music, which is a personal preference and example of God's design and our free will. We can choose what to listen to. If you don't like what is playing on the stereo, change it. Nobody is forcing you to listen to what you are listening to. The point of the analogy is to show the Holy Spirit as the subtle bass and percussion of our soul. If we're not careful, we can cover it with so much other noise that it's drowned out.

Satan's illusion distorts our ability to see clearly, hear crisply, touch tenderly, taste richly and smell distinctly. When our senses are compromised, we become susceptible to deception.

Look at some of the lessons we teach our children to protect them from a pedophile: Don't be lured by candy, don't talk to strangers and never ever get into a strangers car. Think about it. Satan's modus operandi is all about confusing our senses and perception of reality so that what is true about God's design for us is seen as unbelievable.

The quiet whisper of the Holy Spirit is drowned out so we are more susceptible, and the whole notion of God is at the bottom of our list. We become content chasing smoke and mirrors and end up disappointed, depressed, divorced, addicted and suicidal; the only one smiling in the end is the evil one.

The broken world we live in, feeding insatiable appetites without thought or recognizing consequences, the quieting of the inner whisper and creating distance from God is Satan's end game, not an illusion.

Satan's deception is a contrived and synthetic, perfunctory substitute for God's design and too readily accepted in ignorance. We fill ourselves up with counterfeit dreams and empty rhetoric. We buy things we don't need with money we don't have, and the world tells us we've succeeded. We settle for the notion that we are our own god and serve other gods like money, status and success. Our motivations orbit around what we can get, rather than what God has given us to provide others. As twisted as the illusion is, when we recognize it for what it is, we can see through it.

I learned an important lesson as a high school photographer shooting pictures for the school yearbook. The most important tool for the photographer is not in the camera bag, it is in the perspective.

What's your perspective?

There is a significant difference between a snap shot and a photograph. Look at your phone. You can't even buy a phone anymore without a built-in camera. Most phones are equipped with high resolution digital technology, but there is a difference in the quality of the picture beyond pixels. Phone cameras are great to capture a snap shot on the fly, in the moment and impromptu situations. The difference in the artistry of a skilled photographer is in the field of view. There are differences in lighting, contrast, shadow, depth of field, zoom, frame, rule of thirds and lenses that all come into play.

There are differences between shooting silhouettes, close-ups, portraits, action and landscapes, people and animals. The photographer has many tools in the camera bag: lenses, filters, settings, backdrops, but the most important tool is his or her feet— mobility and perspective.

Envision a field of windswept wheat against a flat horizon and a blue, cloudless sky. Imagine taking a picture from a standing position; all the camera sees is where it is pointed. From a standing position, you point and shoot and get a picture without a whole lot going on. There is a line that splits the frame in half vertically with the top half blue and the bottom half a field of wheat. There is not much going on left to right in the picture and really not much subject content.

Since a picture paints a thousand words, the message of the picture could have something to do with vastness or subtle motion. If you look closely, you might be able to see the power of the wind by the direction of the bending wheat. The photograph in and of itself is pretty bland unless the viewer can read into it with some vision and creativity. Consider the picture is taken in black and white without much contrast in lighting, the picture is even blander.

Now let's envision the same setting. The photographer is standing in the same place, but turns 90 degrees to his or her right and the sun comes into view on the horizon. The camera is tilted up a little bit so the sky takes up more than half of the vertical frame. The sun has taken over the upper left corner; the field fills the lower third of the frame, and the horizon slopes downward left to right ending at a fence line curving toward a red barn.

The barn is in the distance with a silo, an old pickup truck and a tractor. Maybe there are a couple horses, chickens and cows; your imagination can fill in the detail of shadows, dissipated light shining down through a few clouds in the blue sky. The red barn is highlighted with white trim glowing in the sun against the deep rich color.

There is a lot more going on in the second picture. There is content, evidence of life, an expectation now that your imagination can look into the picture. There is a difference if the picture was taken at sunrise, noon or sunset. Is the truck coming, going or parked? Maybe if you look closely, you can see a couple enjoying lemonade on the porch of a farmhouse, but for sure there is a dog somewhere.

The reality is that no matter how rich or full or bleak and desperate our life feels now, without the Holy Spirit we are living in the first picture. I can only imagine God's design for us, and His desire provided to Adam and Eve in the garden.

I try to get my head around how great His architectural design, creativity, use of color, texture, attention to detail and quality of craftsmanship is. I fall well short of an adequate expression. To put it into perspective, I begin with what I can see, hear, touch, taste and feel.

Our senses are the inputs to our mind as we experience everything around us; we filter most of it out and focus on what is left as important.

As I'm writing this, I am aware that there is a hum in the background from the air conditioner. I feel the comfort of a cool chill in the air, my lighting is bright enough that my eyes are not strained, and there is no glare on my computer screen. I'm aware that my desk chair is comfortable, the walls of my office have a neutral color, and there is texture of carpet rather than wood floors or concrete.

There is a fragrance in the air that is not made from perfume, air freshener, chemical, food cooking or anything discernible, but there is a fragrance of my surroundings.

Most of this is taken in subconsciously as I focus on what I'm writing to progress the message of the Holy Spirit. If there is an abrupt noise, my attention will be distracted. If the temperature drops and I feel cold, my thoughts will wander to changing the thermostat or changing my clothes.

The same thing happens in the world. I picture a mountain setting with all its majesty, different images in different seasons and times of day. Let's focus on an autumn sunset with snowcapped peaks. The twilight sky is filled with a layer of clouds creating a canvas for God's artistry as the sun sinks behind the mountain. The foreground is a magnificent array of reds, yellows and oranges of autumn leaves. There is a river that runs through prairie grass prior to the mountains accent. There is a chill in the air, and the unique aroma of aspens. Simply said, it is beautiful.

As awe inspiring as the mountain picture can be imagined, how often in our day-to-day life do we recognize God's beauty all around us? We tell ourselves to stop and smell the roses, which is a way the Holy Spirit reminds our spirit that we are losing focus on what's important. Those inner messages have become a part of our modern vernacular.

The imagined mountain landscape is one image, a moment in time, a static view and an individual perspective. We get so busy that we recognize deception and illusion as reality. We look for fulfillment in temporary, immediate gratification and don't see what God offers.

Simply said, with our focus distorted by Satan's illusion, we don't see God. We are confused by Satan's deception and have become blind to God. We have bought into the world perspective and have attempted to package the creator of the universe in a politically correct box palatable for believers without being too offensive to our secular world.

We've missed it: "No eye has seen, no ear has heard, no mind has conceived what God has prepared for those who love him" (1 Corinthians 2:9). It's time for us to wake up and smell the coffee.

Wake up and smell the coffee

GODLESS

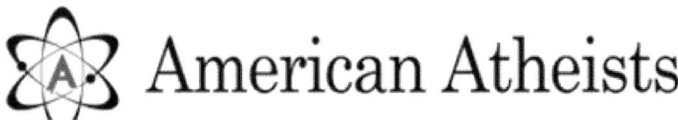 American Atheists

The task of writing about my dream, vision or otherwise experience was approached with prayerful discernment and consideration. My fear of documenting anything of evil that might give root to fertile soil has been consecrated with the sacrificial blood of Christ Jesus. I claim His word and the Armor of God the apostle Paul wrote about in his letter to the people of Ephesus in Ephesians 6:10-18:

Finally, be strong in the Lord and in his mighty power. Put on the full armor of God, so that you can take your stand against the devil's schemes. For our struggle is not against flesh and blood, but against the rulers, against the authorities, against the powers of this dark world and against the spiritual forces of evil in the heavenly realms. Therefore put on the full armor of God, so that when the day of evil comes, you may be able to stand your ground, and after you have done everything, to stand. Stand firm then, with the belt of truth buckled around your waist, with the breastplate of righteousness in place, and with your feet fitted with the readiness that comes from the gospel of peace. In addition to all this, take up the shield of faith, with which you can extinguish all the flaming arrows of the evil one. Take the helmet of salvation and the sword of the Spirit, which is the word of God. And pray in the Spirit on all occasions with all kinds of prayers and requests. With this in mind, be alert and always keep on praying for all the Lord's people.

In so doing, I begin writing of an encounter with the dark world that high-jacked my sleep, paralyzed me with fear and awakened me to the fullness and faithfulness of God Almighty. My recommendation is that you pray to ready yourself prior to reading my account.

Earlier in the evening I had joined some friends at a men's Bible study for fathers, focused on the heart of the father and our Heavenly Father. After the Bible study, I watched a special Billy Graham message on the cross, said goodnight to an otherwise uneventful day and went to bed.

I was awakened by nothing in particular at 2:28 a.m., noticing the time of interrupted sleep, which was a rare occasion. I took advantage of the opportunity to void my bladder and returned to bed shortly after.

I recall being somewhat restless and not returning to sleep quickly. I'm guessing 20-30 minutes later, I drifted off to sleep. I must preface what I'm about to share. I rarely dream or rarely remember dreams when I awake.

The experience of which I write is unlike any dream I've ever had, more vivid and more real than anything I can quantify. I hesitate to even write about it for a few reasons.

First, I don't want people who don't understand or are skeptical of the spiritual realm to think I'm crazy. Second, I'm afraid to revisit my memory of the dream, vision, revelation or whatever it was because it scared me. Third, I don't want to entertain the dark world and the evil one. Finally, I don't have anything to gain, but much to lose if this writing discounts or diminishes the validity or impact of anything else I've written.

So why write at all? First, "You will know the truth, and the truth will set you free" (John 8:32). Second, "Be strong and courageous. Do not be afraid or terrified because of them, for the Lord your God goes with you; he will never leave you nor forsake you" (Deuteronomy 31:6). Third, "You are the light of the world" (Matthew 5:14). Last, "seek first his kingdom and his righteousness, and all these things will be given to you as well" (Matthew 6:33).

So now I'm asleep in bed, and it must have been around 3:00 a.m. I can't really account for the next three hours except to say they included the most realistic subconscious event I've ever experienced.

The dream

I found myself walking in what seemed like an old fairgrounds midway and came upon the Fun House. I didn't need a ticket to get in or anything like that. I just found myself inside. I wasn't with anybody else; I was just walking through a vacant auditorium, stage area or large ballroom. Something about it felt pretend. I knew I was in a Fun House in some sort of carnival and that it wasn't real, but it was very authentic looking in its façade, decoration and realism.

Then I saw the lady of the house and intuitively knew I was in some sort of Reality Theater, test or something of that nature. She was beautiful, sexy and alluring. She was a temptress. Her provocative outfit left little to the imagination.

My first inclination when I saw her was to look away. "Your [My] eyes are too pure to look on evil" (Habakkuk 1:13). In my dream-state, I had a feeling of relief and accomplishment that I had passed the test and advanced beyond the woman. The lingering image of her was more like that of a dominatrix than a seductress, but I had walked on and passed the test.

I now found myself in a hallway where everything seemed run down and dirty. There was a dank and musty smell. The carpet was weathered and torn with exposed wood flooring. The lighting was diffused and erratic like an overhead lamp was swinging. The light and shadows were moving as I proceeded down the hallway.

I was becoming anxious that something or someone was following me. I couldn't see anything but had the feeling of another presence. The walls were closing in on me, and the space was getting tighter. There was a foul smell of urine mixed with an acrid stench of blood and burnt gun powder. My apprehension built, and I began to look for a way out.

Then I came into a room that had walls of mirrors—not flat, framed mirrors that you could see yourself in, but Fun House mirrors that distorted your reflection. Only these mirrors looked dirty and didn't show a reflection of me but a reflection of humanity as if I were looking into something with contempt, disgust and repulsion. The mirrors were more like windows, but the images were not human or even animal like. They were iridescent, shape changing, chameleon demons.

I realize definitively that I don't want to see anymore. My heart is racing, and I'm tired of this test or demonstration. I'm pleased again with myself that I wasn't drawn in, but I'm done and really want to get out.

I see a sign that says "Keep Out." Somehow in my haste, I think it's a "real" sign—part of the Fun House is closed for maintenance or something, and I peek in. The room looks empty with the exception of a step ladder and a drop cloth with some tools and equipment on the floor.

I step inside thinking I might find an emergency exit. As soon as I've cleared the threshold, the door closes behind me with a vacuum seal, and it's suddenly quiet. In that instant, I knew the door behind me was gone, there was no turning back, and I had stepped into some serious excrement. There were several things happening at the same time.

The smells and silence hit me simultaneously. I can't describe what it sounds like to be completely deaf, but I have a new appreciation for what silence is. All the Febreze in the world and a floral shop couldn't mask the foul, rotten egg, sulfur and outhouse smell. It was then I realized that I was completely paralyzed, frozen in place. I couldn't move anything but my eyes.

It was more than not being able to move; paralysis comes with loss of feeling. I could feel everything with heightened tactile appreciation from the inside out. My veins were filled with something like mercury or molasses, something dense and heavy—not blood. My breathing was labored as if I was trying to suck air out of an empty scuba tank, and my chest was heavy. I was aware that I was standing, yet I couldn't step, bend, lean, twist or twitch.

I was facing what looked like a picture on the wall, but I couldn't make out the content of the composition. It looked like bundles of twigs or rope-like vines and a thicket of branches. As I tried to focus to make out what the imagery in the picture was, it began to move.

The content within the frame started to squirm like a body of snakes or human-like intestines. Only they were covered with a tree-like bark or leathery skin that was rough like bark, when I realized it was more like charred flesh, scabbed over breaking and oozing as it moved. Some of them began to take on human shape and form, and then they began to sink into the wall like sand through an hour glass.

The void area began to consume the area around it. All I wanted to do was look away, but I could not. I'd lost control of my eyes, the ability to move or blink had been taken away. All I could do was watch until it consumed me with its implosion. I was literally sucked into a black hole. All my tactile senses were gone, but my thoughts and equilibrium were intact. Now I have a sense of what a spirit feels like, but I was not in control of its movement.

I knew beyond all reason that I was not where I was supposed to be, something had gone horribly wrong. What was happening was a violation of the Most High. I desperately wanted to wake up but I couldn't. Try as I might, I felt myself being swept, whisked and slurped away. I was caught up in the current around me accelerating with its intensity far beyond terminal velocity. There was nothing I could do on my own to stop or get out. I could not wake myself from this dream state.

I could sense that I was approaching the point of no return and cried out, "Get behind me Satan; I rebuke you in the name of my Lord Jesus Christ!" I screamed for my life, knowing that I was protected and ransomed with the blood of Christ. "'Satan, you are rebuked!' And they [I] overcame him by the blood of the Lamb, and by the word of their [my] testimony" (Revelations 12:11).

I was spiritually awakened literally and figuratively and rescued from my episode a few minutes before 6:00 a.m. The episode could have lasted a few seconds, minutes or hours. There is no reasonable explanation to me why I had this experience. All I know is that His word states, "And we know that in all things God works for the good of those who love him, who have been called according to his purpose" (Romans 8:28).

So in that, if my testimony of this experience helps glorify Him as an example of the reality of spiritual warfare, the importance of the Armor of God and His unfailing faithfulness, I can rest in the peace of His comfort. Jehovah Shalom.

Satan's Illusion

- Satan – prince of the earth
- The world – sets the standard
- Body – serve the flesh
- Mind – you only live once
- Inner Spirit – whatever feels good
- Holy Spirit – is a fantasy
- God – make believe

GOD'S REALITY

"God saw all that he had made, and it was very good. And there was evening, and there was morning—the sixth day" (Genesis 1:31).

We've all heard sayings like, "The early bird gets the worm" and "early to rise makes a man healthy, wealthy and wise." Yet we make habits out of late nights at the office, pulling all-nighters cramming for an exam or turning last call into a breakfast meeting. We sleep in when given the chance and are literally and figuratively asleep at the wheel.

Look at all the books written for self-help and success in business that have something to do with focus, mission, vision, strategy and changing your paradigm.

The first part of this book set the framework for our perspective and worldview based on deception of Satan's illusion. When the illusion is revealed, the operative questions are, "What is the truth?" "What is the reality of why we were created in the first place?" "What does God want us to do?"

I'm not a theologian or Bible scholar, but I was taught how to read and write and learned about the "Five Ws and the H" in elementary school: who, what, where, when, why and how. Every good story contains these key elements so let's go to God's Word, the Bible, and unpack the story.

"In the beginning, God created the heavens and the earth" (Genesis 1:1). The first ten words of the Bible contain the essential elements for every story ever written. Every book ever written, every story ever told must contain these elements to transfer knowledge through oration and written language to convey anything of meaning.

Five Ws and the H: Who? God. What? Created. When? In the beginning. Where? Heavens and the Earth. Why? Key question ... we'll get to that. How? God spoke it. "God said, let there be light" (Genesis 1:3).

I think it's interesting that we pull all-nighters and wander around in darkness just like the world did before God created the heavens and the earth. "The earth was formless and void ... and God said, let there be light" (Genesis 1:2-3). When you think about it, we are like the world that way, kept in the dark until we accept God's light.

We just spent several pages exploring Satan's deception and the affect illusion has on our perspective of the world we live in. Deception is a lie that you believe to be true, and Satan is the ultimate deceiver. He creates enticing scenarios, creatively positioned opportunities designed specifically to match your secret desires.

If God didn't create us to be Satan's play toy or entertainment, then why did God create us, and what are we designed for? "God created man in His own image, in the image of God He created him; male and female He created them" (Genesis 1:27).

Our sole purpose was to glorify Him. "Let the Lord be glorified (Isaiah 66:5). "I will give thanks to thee, O Lord my God, with all my heart, and glorify thy name forever (Psalm 86:12).

Jesus teaches us in the gospel according to Matthew, "Let your light shine before men in such a way that they may see your good works, and glorify your father who is in heaven" (Matthew 5:16).

When Jesus' time on earth was drawing to an end, He gave them (His disciples) a new commandment, "that you love one another, even as I have loved you" (John 13:34). We were created to glorify Him, and we do that by loving others. He gave us everything we need to be fruitful and multiply for His glory, and the rest is history.

A divine purpose

Our entire history is His story. He created mankind to glorify Him, yet we lacked obedience and self control and fell short of the mark. The Bible is not some dusty old ancient text; it's a murder mystery, an epic drama, a war saga. There's a villain and a hero, an oppressed people, underdogs, plot twists, murder, intrigue, deceit, rape, murder, parables, miracles and resurrection. There is romance, poetry, prophecy and fulfillment.

The Old Testament is the gospel concealed, and the gospel is the Old Testament exposed in a mystery revealed. The mystery really becomes my story, because Jesus died on the cross for each and every one of us individually.

We were knit together in our mother's womb for a divine purpose. We get distracted by what the world demands from us to feel comfortable and succeed. Most of us have accepted a discounted perspective of what life is about and strive only to survive mediocrity. We work to survive and never really live. Our dreams have been substituted with lies of what we need to be happy.

It all sounds good to begin with. Who can argue with teachings to be nice, do well in school, study hard, get good grades, graduate, get a job, fall in love, get married, buy a house, raise a family, secure a retirement, be comfortable and leave a legacy of an inheritance when you die? Remember, the enemy seeks only to steal, kill and destroy.

Imagine how different life would be if you were doing what the creator of the universe intended for you. I'm not suggesting that all of the things listed above aren't important; they are just out of order. God should be first. Matthew 6:33 can change your life: "Seek ye first the kingdom of God and His righteousness and all these things shall be added unto you." What Jesus is referring to in this verse, where He says "all these things," are all those things we look to for security instead of trusting Him.

This section of Scripture is the "Don't worry be happy" message. The birds don't have a home, but they have a place to sleep. They do not have clothes, but they are covered with feathers. They don't have a pantry, but they have food.

He shows us repeatedly all over nature that His creative ability is beyond our comprehension. With all of the technology at our disposal, we simply cannot create anything out of nothing. He did.

I love this quote by Howard Thurman: "Don't ask yourself what the world needs. Ask what makes you come alive, and go do it. Because what the world needs is people who have come alive" (thinkexist.com).

When we seek God's will for us and are obedient to fulfill that calling, we will find what makes us come alive. God is faithful, and you can trust Him; He won't give you a vision of the destination and not equip you for the journey. "So whether you eat or drink or whatever you do, do it all for the glory of God" (1 Corinthians 10:31).

HOLY SPIRIT

Peter replied,
"Repent and be baptized, every one of you,
in the name of Jesus Christ for the
forgiveness of your sins. And you will
receive the gift of the Holy Spirit"
(Acts 2:38).

Imagine that you've never been on an airplane, but you've always been interested in flying. You would see birds flying and subconsciously think how cool that would be. You can imagine taking flight whenever you wanted and go anywhere, at any time. You could rise above the distractions and clutter around you and see things from a whole new perspective. You could rise above the buildings and the trees, navigate well above any construction, detours and obstacles of the road to create the best path from here to there.

The most direct path between two points is a straight line, and you could fly between A and B without deviation.

As exciting as that would be, you realize that you are not a bird and the only way to fly is with a plane or glider of some sort. An airplane sounds like the most viable solution for you to experience flight, so you start to explore your options. You could take a commercial flight and combine the experience with a little vacation or sightseeing flight.

It's not so much that you need to get anywhere specifically, so departure and arrival aren't really the issue. You just want to experience what it is like to fly.

Sightseeing sounds pretty practical, and then somebody mentions skydiving. All of a sudden something goes off in you like, "Yeah, that's it, that's the ticket."

You are a little scared because you've never even been on a plane, let alone even thought about jumping out of a perfectly good one.

The thought of it stays with you. You begin to notice people skydiving in your day-to-day experiences. Suddenly you're aware of skydiving in the movies and on TV. The phenomenon is similar to buying a car you intend to be somewhat unique and after you purchase it, realize that it's not the only one. You see pictures of people skydiving in magazines. You see a sign along the highway ... literally. There is a billboard that simply says 1 800 SKY-DIVE.

You decide to go for it and remember an old saying, "You only live once," right?

So the day comes. You've taken the ground school classes and understand how the equipment works. You've been instructed what to do in case of emergency and how to roll out of a hard landing. You are a little bit scared, but more excited than afraid. You can see the plane as you walk across the tarmac. The skin of the aircraft looks sleek and fast. As you get closer, you can hear the roar of the engine, feel the wind created by the engine and smell jet fuel and hydraulic fluid so thick in the air you can taste it. There are only a few steps on the rolling stairway to climb, and you board the plane.

Once you're on board, you realize that the plane isn't as spacious as it looked from the outside. You expected something more like one of those custom jets you'd seen in the movies, one with all the comforts and trimmings. Then you realize this flight's only function is to get you off the ground with no frills attached. After all, you don't plan to land in it anyway. You ask yourself, *Who in their right mind jumps out of a perfectly good airplane?* You've heard others ask that question rhetorically, but suddenly the question becomes real.

The pilot is cleared for take-off, and you can feel the plane begin to accelerate. The plane bumps and sways as it picks up speed down the runway. There is an instant where speed turns to flight, and you are in the air. The plane's wings pitch and move, searching for wind and lift as you begin your accent. You look out a small window and watch your perceptions change as things on the ground begin to lose size. You've begun to settle into the flight to relax for a moment, and the jump master asks you if you are ready to skydive.

Your mouth says "Yes," while your mind and body are reluctant to follow. Yet you proceed as you were instructed and move into position. There are hand holds and foot rests attached to the plane's wing. You know the hand holds are waiting for you to grab hold of them.

The noise of the wind rushing by is deafening; its power attempts to pull you out of the plane. As you reach for the hand hold, wind resistance obstructs your hand from going where you want it to go, much like a child sticking his hand out the window of a speeding car surfing the air current as it goes by.

You are committed to the jump and move into position on the wing of the plane. There is no going back. It would be more dangerous to go back than to surrender to the fall. In your mind, you give yourself a three count: one, two, three …. You loosen your grip, which initiates a chain of events nothing can stop. The laws of physics take over, and the pull of gravity separates you from the plane.

In the same moment, you realize you are falling. Your body instinctively wants to tuck into a fetal position protecting its internal organs, but your mind overrides the natural tendency of cover. You arch your back and spread your arms and legs as you were instructed. In this moment, you are as vulnerable as you have ever been and you continue to fall.

Adrenaline pumps as you continue to fall. The feeling is unlike an elevator dropping away or the downward drop of a rollercoaster. Adrenaline is a unique chemical the brain produces, which enables the body to perform extraordinary tasks in difficult situations. We've all heard stories of people lifting cars or doing miraculous and heroic things with assistance from adrenaline.

You are accelerating through your extended feeling of falling, and adrenaline is pumping while you're falling—accelerating and pumping adrenaline into nooks and crannies of your brain and body that only few people experience.

The acceleration of your fall continues until you reach terminal velocity of approximately 120 mph, and you realize that you are being supported by a cushion of air.

This is freefall, and adrenaline continues to pump throughout your fall. You get a read on your descent by looking at your altimeter, which tells when the desired altitude is reached and it's time to pull the rip cord. All goes well and your parachute opens, the canopy fully deploys as it was designed so that you can enjoy the rest of your descent until you are safely returned to the ground.

Putting God first

Your senses are heightened for days after this experience due to the influx of adrenaline into your body chemistry. You experience improved clarity around critical decision making, acute vision, enhanced hearing and near photographic memory I refer to as the *awareness factor*.

The Holy Spirit is God's way to be tangible in us like adrenaline works in the skydiver. The Holy Spirit is God's way to be a part of us. "For we through the spirit, by faith, are waiting for the hope of righteousness" (Galatians.5:5).

The acts of the flesh are obvious

When we put God first instead of feeding the flesh to accommodate Satan's illusion, we are redeemed. Galatians 5:19-23:

The acts of the flesh are obvious: sexual immorality, impurity and debauchery; idolatry and witchcraft; hatred, discord, jealousy, fits of rage, selfish ambition, dissensions, factions and envy; drunkenness, orgies, and the like. I warn you, as I did before, that those who live like this will not inherit the kingdom of God. But the fruit of the Spirit is love, joy, peace, forbearance, kindness, goodness, faithfulness, gentleness and self-control. Against such things there is no law.

When we put God first, we become filled with the Holy Spirit, which comes to us in many forms: Jehovah-Jireh, our provider (Philippians 4:19), Jehovah-Nissi, victorious (John 16:33), Jehovah-Rohi, shepherd (Psalm 23), Jehovah-Shammah, omni-present (Matthew 28:19-20), Jehovah-Shalom, peace-comforter (Ephesians 2:14), Jehovah-M'Kaddesh, sanctifier (John 17:17-19), Jehovah-Rophe, healer (Mark 1:34) and Jehovah-Tsidkenu, righteousness (1 John 1:1-2).

As we put God first, the Holy Spirit becomes comingled with our own spirit and guides our thoughts and actions. We commonly refer to this as our conscience.

If you've ever had *that feeling* you should go ahead and do something, then discover you are glad you did; or had *that feeling* you shouldn't do something but went ahead and did it anyway, you know what I'm talking about.

We all know that feeling, whether you are a practicing Christian or not; just like it doesn't really matter to God if you believe in Him or not. He knows He exists with or without our acceptance, and eternity is in the balance depending on our choice—but we all know *that feeling*.

We refer to it basically as your gut feeling. What does your gut say? gut check. "Since what may be known about God is plain to them, because God has made it plain to them. For since the creation of the world God's invisible qualities—his eternal power and divine nature—have been clearly seen, being understood from what has been made, so that people are without excuse" (Romans 1:19-20).

THE INNER SPIRIT

"I pray that out of his glorious riches he may strengthen you with power through his Spirit in your inner being" (Ephesians 3:16).

Once you profess your belief in the fact that Jesus is the Son of God, that He died for you, was buried and rose again, you become "made new," "born again," "Child of God," a "Christian." The Holy Spirit comes into your heart and resides in your inner most being, the way God intended it to be. You become whole, in Christ.

That God-shaped hole, the emptiness, the feeling that there's got to be more to life than the world standard, more than the status quo, more than getting by and getting ahead until you're dead, is filled with the Holy Spirit.

Let's talk about the spirit, living in the spirit, allowing the Holy Spirit to comingle with your inner being. When I think of the inner spirit and feeling that completeness, it keeps bringing me back to the *awareness factor* and the conditions that need to be in place to experience it. It all starts with seeking Him first, right?

Matthew 6:33, that is the cornerstone of Seek Ye First Ministries and where it all began for me. Jeremiah 29:13 says, "You will seek me and find me when you seek me with all of your heart." When our heart meets Jesus in the sweet spot of the cross, something spiritual takes place. We are made new and become a child of God.

We can hear His voice. Jesus uses stories to teach us about the good shepherd and His flock of sheep and how they hear His voice. "My sheep know my voice and hear my call."

He also talks of healing the deaf and giving vision to the blind. There's a spiritual healing that takes place for our ears to hear the voice of God's call for us and for our eyes to have clarity to pierce the enemy's veil of illusion and to see the truth. His voice becomes a lamp to our feet and a light to our path when we follow Him, making us whole.

The sweet-spot of the cross

There is so much hurt in the world, and everybody seems to be yearning for something more. We have an inner desire to feel complete or being made whole.

There's a touching scene in the 1996 movie "Jerry Maguire." Jerry returns home from a long trip of missed opportunities and broken dreams to reclaim his wife. He finds her in the midst of a support group of divorced women and pleads for her love leading up to the famous line: "You complete me."

Then everyone sheds a tear when Renee Zellweger's character, Dorothy Boyd, says, "You had me at hello."

This feeling of completeness is what I refer to as the *awareness factor*. It's the sweet spot of being aware of God's presence evident in you and realizing His impact through you in the world around you. God shows up in a lot of unexpected ways and part of the relationship is to recognize His work, praise Him and to be grateful. When we're aware of His presence, it's a beautiful thing.

But we live compromised by sin, weighed down by guilt and shame. We try harder to earn our way to something better. Left to our own devices, we are inadequate, but God is the differentiator. If we seek Him first, listen to His voice and are obedient to follow His lead, we put the rest of the process in alignment to be aware of His presence and make a difference in the world around us.

Let me try to illustrate this through a story. I had the epiphany that Jesus was who He said He was and that all of it—the Bible, the resurrection, being adopted into God's family, being made whole, a new creation, a royal priest, eternal life—was the truth. When truth hits you, that changes how you respond when somebody cuts you off in traffic or you see somebody on the side of the road in need of a meal.

Over time, this realization changes how I interact with the world around me. I began to pursue knowledge of God's will for my life and prayed for courage to carry it out. That's where this whole idea of a ministry initiative came together around Matthew 6:33-34: "But, seek first the kingdom of God and His righteousness and all these things shall be given to you as well. Therefore do not worry about tomorrow, for tomorrow will worry about itself. Each day has enough trouble of its own."

Seek Ye First Ministries became my mission to carry the message to encourage others to put God first.

The letters SYF became a logo that represents the message of the gospel and the resurrection with the Father, Son and Holy Spirit coming out of the tomb represented by the circle. SYF: Seek, Ye, First. Then it came to me—SYF: Share Your Faith.

I wanted to start a movement; I wanted to change the world one conversation at a time; I wanted SYF to be synonymous with revival in America and for Christians all over the world to wear SYF and be prepared to share a message about their faith.

See how easily this became about me?: "I wanted," "I wanted …."

I didn't realize it, but I wanted to be glorified by what I was doing for God's kingdom: how many people I could convert through sharing His message and telling others about the life changes He was making in my life. It became about me, in some way showing God how worthy I was to earn a place in His kingdom. I had it all wrong.

Relationships

It's not about what "we want"; it's about relationship. He knows the desires of our heart since He created us. There's nothing we can do to make God love us any more than He does, and nothing we've done can separate us from His love. We were created out of love, and we glorify Him by loving others.

What are you searching for? Have you asked the questions: "Why am I here?" "What's my purpose?" "What's God's will for me?"

When we start to ask those questions, we allow His Spirit to begin a relationship with our inner being. I think of it like some kind of spiritual dance, where His Spirit leads and I follow. I keep stepping on His toes, He has to set me up straight, and I need to yield to follow His lead. There is intimacy in the dance. There's a relationship that develops when He leads and I follow.

THE MIND

"Do not conform to the pattern of this world, but be transformed by the renewing of your mind. Then you will be able to test and approve what God's will is—his good, pleasing and perfect will" (Romans 12:2).

"I Can Only Imagine" is a song made popular by Mercy Me. The song lyrics include imagining *what it will be like ... surrounded by your (God's) glory, what will my heart feel? Will I dance for you Jesus? Or in awe of you be still? Will I stand in your presence? Or to my knees will I fall? Will I sing hallelujah? Or will I be able to speak at all? I can only imagine ....*

Our mind is a powerful tool, a gift from God and an integral part of His design specification for us, created in His image.

The dictionary defines "mind" as a noun: "(in a human or other conscious being) the element, part, substance, or process that reasons, thinks, feels, wills, perceives, judges, etc.: *the processes of the human mind*" (Dictionary.com).

"Do not conform to the pattern of this world, but be transformed by the renewing of your mind. Then you will be able to test and approve what God's will is—his good, pleasing and perfect will" (Romans 12:2).

We are born land based people, earth dwellers; yet we consist of and require water to live. However, we cannot breathe in an aquatic environment once we are birthed into air.

Imagine the heat of a desert landscape, sun-baked sand, dry arid heat scorching your lungs when you breathe and all you can see is a sparingly decorated horizon of cactus. Now feel the sand between your toes and suddenly you are transported to a tropical beach with palm trees, the fragrance and humidity of salt air surrounded by azure blue waters, warmed by the sun and the sounds of the waves lapping the beach.

Two thirds of the earth's surface is covered with water and all you need are goggles to explore what's beneath the surface, but it takes training and specialized equipment to experience breathing underwater. You've been prepared with all the training, have all the equipment and tools and find comfort in experiencing the weightlessness of neutral buoyancy and to breathe underwater. Once you are submerged and realize that you don't have to hold your breath, the aquatic environment takes on a new dimension.

The underwater world takes on new meaning as you experience it from beneath the water's surface. Fish do not swim away from you as if you are an intruder but swim alongside with you. Your breathing is effortless as you ride along a gentle current at a comfortable depth surrounded by water as you pass living coral, plants, and fish too numerous to count. It's like you are flying without the need for wings or any physical propulsion, just floating and absorbing everything around you—and it is good.

What are your gifts?

God's design is that the Holy Spirit resides within us and is at work with our inner spirit, which directs the thoughts of our mind and the actions of our body. When our thoughts and actions are properly aligned with God's will, we are functioning as designed. Simply put, we think before we act—not the other way around.

Most of the damage control, clean up, treatment, therapy, counseling, etc. would be prevented if people checked their alignment routinely as you should on a car. God provides the gift of discernment, which is wisdom and decision making; we are not simply genetic matter existing purely for survival. We have a purpose. The purpose of God's design is to utilize the talents, gifts, creativity, etc. to glorify Him through our thoughts and actions. In turn, we will be blessed with abundant life here on earth.

We all have to do our part.

I recall as a young athlete that I migrated more to individual than team sports as a result of having a call reversed in a Little League championship football game. I experienced the thrill of victory and the agony of defeat within seconds of each other as my touchdown run didn't count. The game clock ran out and the season was over, just like that.

It wasn't that I didn't like being part of a team—far from it. I could mentally prepare myself for my piece of the puzzle and enjoyed sharing in the result of good teamwork. I just didn't like the burden of being the piece of critical failure in team execution.

A chain is only as strong as its weakest link and all that. In a team sport, everybody had to execute their part with impact and precision timing for the desired result.

In an individual sport, I would only let myself down if I didn't execute according to plan.

People meditate on various aspects of life. It's how we listen to God. As a young gymnast, I would close my eyes and picture flawless execution of the vault, parallel bars, pommel horse or tumbling routine. We had a really good high bar and rings squad, so I wasn't an "all-around" gymnast.

The point is that through mental discipline, practice and repetition, the body learns the routine and muscle memory. In gymnastics, there are so many "little things" to think about. For example: point your toes, extend, stay tight, legs together, don't arch, balance, hold, explode … everything required precise timing or it would spell disaster.

Mental preparation, practice and repetition help develop muscle memory for the physical activity, which is the beginning of the process.

There are many figures of speech that remind us of this: keep your eye on the ball, keep your head in the game and made famous by Bill Murray in "Caddy Shack," "be the ball" are just a few examples.

"Get Your Head in the Game" was a song made popular in Disney's movie "High School Musical." I watched it when my girls were younger. Focus, determination and mental preparation come into play whether it's gymnastics, golf, karate, football … every physical event of activity is only partially physical; the rest is mental.

The body does what the mind tells it to do. Granted there are activities so routine like breathing that happen without conscious thought, but basically the body does what the mind thinks of doing.

I remember riding on the bus to gymnastics meets before everybody had iPods and head sets. We would close our eyes and think through our routines for the various events. You would mentally prepare for every nuance of every trick in the routine. When you mentally placed yourself in the moment of the situation and could envision it through, the outcome was always better.

We would have looked funny to anyone who didn't know what the pommel horse squad was doing when they used two fingers as imaginary legs "walking through" a horse routine with their fingers. This helped visualize the routine and solidify the mental preparation. The expectation was when you visualized the flawless routine, physical execution would improve.

Putting God first

The reality is when we put God first, recognize the Holy Spirit within us and think through our actions prior to acting, we get better results. YOLO takes on a whole new meaning when you recognize that we really do only live once and our one time lasts forever.

The split second decisions we make on the fly have impacts affecting our eternity. We make thousands of little decisions every day; we better be careful what we put into motion with our body. What we think in our mind guides the body into action.

As Christians, we talk about a leap of faith. I like to think of it more like a skydiver surrendering all and making the jump. In order to experience the thrill of falling through the sky, accelerating to terminal velocity and freefall, you must jump out of a perfectly good airplane.

Earlier we looked at how adrenaline works in the skydiver and creates the effect I called the *awareness factor*. "Set your minds on things above, not on earthly things" (Colossians 3:2). When we put God first, utilize the Holy Spirit to guide our mind, and make decisions accordingly, we are in alignment with His will for us. The proper alignment of our spirit, mind and body with God and the Holy Spirit results in our ability to perform as designed, live abundantly and glorify Him.

I was thinking about the paradigm shift required in how I think or how we should think as Christians. Our natural tendency is to care about what others think, how we look, what's politically correct and how we fit in. Our propensity to seek approval from an early age leads to anxiety, depression, and addiction in too many instances as the result of feelings of abandonment or our inability to integrate into something bigger.

This is Satan's strategy to divide and conquer, derailing us from God's design for us to follow His will and glorify Him. The great deceiver is pretty successful in this strategy; look around you.

So literally, I looked around me as I was riding a bus, contemplating the paradigm shift required, or as my girls would say, "zoning out." Not really paying attention to anything around me, I looked out the window and saw a billboard fleeting by. The billboard's message was straightforward and simply said, "Change Your Mind, Change Your Life."

That's it! Unmistakably, this was a sign from God. The billboard wasn't even mounted alongside the highway; it was behind an industrial building, across the frontage road, in the back of a parking lot, on a trailer and I happened to see it.

Coincidences really don't exist in my perspective of the world. I call them God-instances and see more of them when I'm focused on God's will and my situational awareness is increased—another example of the *awareness factor*.

"The wise man's eyes are in his head, but the fool walks in darkness" (Ecclesiastes 2:14).

THE BODY

"And God placed all things under his feet and appointed him to be head over everything for the church, which is his body, the fullness of him who fills everything in every way" (Ephesians 1:22-23).

Recall the earlier metaphor of the motor, "Get Your Motor Running" by Steppenwolf. It's easy to picture a motorcycle or car. For purposes of this discussion, let's think in terms of a car.

The Holy Trinity: God the Father, Jesus the Son, and the Holy Spirit. We are created in His image with mind, body and spirit. We were created, His design—simply to bring Him glory in all we do. "Before all people I will be glorified" (Leviticus 10:3). He gave us everything we would ever need to accomplish this simple task.

However, we read in Exodus the story of Moses and leading the Israelites out of bondage in Egypt. The Lord came to Moses and at first Moses must have been asking the Lord, "Me? Seriously, you really want me?" See, Moses wasn't in a position of leadership with his people. The fact is that Moses was a fugitive, a murderer.

In today's vernacular, he'd be a wanted man, a criminal, a bad guy. No wonder people say the Lord works in mysterious ways. Not only does the Lord choose Moses to lead the Israelites out of Egypt, but He doesn't make it easy for Moses. "I will harden Pharaoh's heart, and he will pursue them [the Israelites]. But I will gain glory for myself through Pharaoh and all his army, and the Egyptians will know that I am the LORD" (Exodus 14:4).

Stay with me here, I know I'm talking collectively of God's chosen people. We'll get into our individual bodies shortly, but this is important. He chose Moses, a normal man, a bad guy, to lead His chosen people the Israelites out of Egypt. Why? "I will harden Pharaoh's heart, and he will pursue them" [the Israelites]. Then, "I will gain glory for myself through Pharaoh and all his army." Why? "The Egyptians will know that I am the Lord" (Exodus 14:4).

We spent several pages illustrating how Satan deceives us and tries to steal, kill and destroy us along the way. This is God's way of showing us that we don't have to take it anymore. We can break free from the bondage of slavery as the Israelites did, and we can break free from the bondage Satan throws at us in the form of materialism, addiction and sin.

Ask yourself which is a more compelling story: God gives Moses a winning lottery ticket, and he buys his way through the wilderness with a first class ticket, or there is a dramatic battle of the Israelites breaking free from generations of bondage and slavery from Egypt?

Pharaoh has a hardened heart. God's afflicted Pharaoh and his people with plague after plague. God got personal and killed Pharaoh's first born and the first born of the next generation of his people.

It's not like Moses just walked up to Pharaoh and said, "We want to go; my people and I are getting kind of tired of putting up with all this bondage stuff, so … can you just let my people go?" Can you imagine Pharaoh saying, "Yeah, that's cool. You guys can go. Don't forget to take all your goats and stuff."

That would not have made a very compelling testimony of perseverance and endurance. It would not have been a story about belief, faith, trust and hope. It had to be difficult for there to be a story of deliverance; no pain, no gain.

Well, we're the same as individuals. Look at the movies we respond to; the one's that move us. Hollywood has picked up on the fact that everyone likes a plot. There has to be some conflict, a villain and a hero, an underdog to root for. The story would be pretty boring to watch if the protagonist (good guy or girl) just went through life one day at a time with nothing to overcome, nothing to drive him or her to search for something more or improve.

"The Truman Show," a movie with Jim Carey, was released in 1998. Carey plays Truman Burbank, who lives in a reality show surrounded by actors, filmed since his birth. Everything in Truman's life is scripted and mundane until there is a glitch in the technology exposing a weakness in his world. These struggles define us as a people and as a being.

Made in God's image

As Christians, we are adopted into God's family, becoming His children, which make up the body of His church, the bride of Christ. Collectively, we play a part in the larger story where we are called to love one another as Christ loves us, and individually we are called to love our enemy as God loves us. It's easy to lose sight that we belong to something bigger than ourselves. The old play from our enemy is to divide and conquer.

We look at ourselves as individuals and become a body of self-centered, opportunistic individuals needing to differentiate ourselves to get ahead. The world rewards hard work at an individual level, and it's natural to be consumed with ourselves and our body and self-image; we become god of self.

If we make it personal, it's about our body. We're all made in God's image, with infinite creativity at His disposal; no two of us are alike. How cool is that? Well I guess that depends on how your package came out of assembly. Some were gifted with an appearance that appeals to others. Some see this as a blessing, while others see it as a curse. Either way, God created us to be us and our bodies are a vessel; it matters how we treat our bodies.

As I write, I'm reminded of information technology and the computer adage "Garbage in, garbage out." It's true of how we treat our bodies. I'm convicted where I sit that I've been complacent with my health. I like to say that I've matured out of my old jeans when they no longer fit. The hard truth is I haven't made time to exercise, eat healthy, and I'm responsible for the weight gain.

The question we can go to God with of our body is, *Are we using it to glorify Him?* When I think of that question and comparisons of how I look and my body image compared to my brothers and others, it fails in response to the question with God. *Where are you taking His body?*

I'm reminded of the lyrics in the Danny Gokey song, "More Than You Think I Am":

You always think I'm somewhere on a mountain top
But never think behind bars
You'd be amazed at places that I'd go to be with you Where you are.

As much as our body is a vessel that can be taken places, we are also responsible for what we put in it. I lack discipline and self-control when it comes to ice cream and mini-donuts. We think of abuse in terms of what people do to others, but what about the abuse we do to ourselves? The evidence is all around us with obesity, alcoholism and drug addiction.

THE WORLD

"The earth is the Lord's, and everything in it, the world, and all who live in it" (Psalm 24:1).

"He's got the whole world, in His hands …." Remember that song? The one who created it all: "God saw all that He had made and said it is very good. And there was evening, and there was morning—the sixth day" (Genesis 1:31).

He created it for us to use to glorify Him. Then we broke ties with our creator and have labored on our own, separated from God through sin, and the prince of darkness has ruled the earth.

It's not difficult to see when we look around that things are out of control. In a sense, they have been out of order since the garden. God's chosen people have been persecuted since Abraham, Isaac and Jacob through Joseph and David, and Christians have been persecuted since Jesus went to the cross. We don't have to look very far to see a headline or story in the news about something gone bad in the world.

There's corruption and scandal in every neighborhood and every country from the farm house to the courthouse. We live in a world that is moving so fast that we need posters to tell us to stop and smell the roses or apps to remind us to get up and walk around. Our enemy has created a world of distractions, which reminds me of smoke and mirrors used by the stage illusionists. The illusionist distracts the audience with noise, glitz and glamour, so they don't see the truth of what's happening.

Jesus teaches us to "seek first the kingdom of God" (Matthew 6:33) and says, "You are the light of the world. A town built on a hill cannot be hidden" (Matthew 5:14). "Do not be deceived" (Galatians 6:7).

We're instructed to "Trust in the Lord with all your heart and lean not on your own understanding; in all your ways submit to Him, and He will make your paths straight" (Proverbs 3 5-6). "Your word is a lamp for my feet and a light on my path" (Psalm 119:105).

Comfort zone

Earlier I wrote about the *awareness factor* and a kind of spiritual dance. Like a tango, the dance is intimate, personal and all part of the relationship-building process—establishing trust. I see this process illustrated though Psalm 119:105. I pray for knowledge of His will for me and courage to carry it out. He calls me out of my comfort zone to take a step. His word becomes a lamp to my feet and a light to my path. When I trust Him, I take a step, then He calls me to another and so it goes. The two-step tango of my spiritual walk. The pace and purpose of the walk increases as our relationship grows.

Jesus instructs His followers to "go and make disciples of all nations, baptizing them in the name of the Father and of the Son and of the Holy Spirit" (Matthew 28:19). Our purpose is to glorify Him, and we can do that by making disciples, which starts at home, in our neighborhood, and where we work.

It's not about how much you do; it's about what He can do through you when you submit your will and are available for His use. He created you for a time such as this, and He can use you where you are. There's nothing we can do to have Him love us anymore, but this is no game.

As a kid, I remember playing in the woods behind my elementary school that bordered the Minnesota River valley separating two southern suburbs of Minneapolis. I always wondered what it would have been like to live in the time before roads and bridges that connected the two neighboring areas. My friends and I would play for hours in those woods after school and on weekends.

There was an area in the woods called Nine Mile Creek. On a few occasions, we would assemble enough kids to play Capture the Flag.

We would divide into two teams; each team had its own territory defined with agreed upon boundaries, separated by the creek. Each team had a flag and could place it anywhere in their territory. The objective of the game was to capture the other team's flag, which meant players from each team had to enter the opposing team's area to steal the flag and return it to their own side.

Your team could defend the flag and capture intruders, putting them in "jail." We had variations of the rules depending on who was playing and how much time we had. Sometimes you could escape from "jail," sometimes you had to be rescued, and sometimes you stayed in "jail" until the game was over.

The game ended when one team captured the opponent's flag and returned it safely to their area. Each team would develop its own strategy, and players were chosen for their speed, athleticism and even stealth capabilities.

I always wanted to be the kid who went into the enemy camp to capture the flag, but you had to find it first. There was always a risk for the explorers to be captured and "jailed." Once the flag was located, it was important to wait in the shadows for the opportune time to strike. Then it was an all-out race to get back to your side to win the game.

"Enemy occupied territory that is what this world is. Christianity is the story of how the rightful king has landed, you might say landed in disguise, and is calling us to take part in a great campaign of sabotage."
C.S. Lewis – "Mere Christianity"

"Enemy occupied territory." The Bible calls believers "aliens" and "foreigners" in our own land. When we're adopted into the kingdom of God as His children, we become residents of heaven. From the Lord's prayer: "Your kingdom come, your will be done on earth as it is in heaven" (Matthew 6:10). "Now if we are children, then we are heirs—heirs of God and co-heirs with Christ" (Romans 8:17).

We are heirs to the kingdom, but we are not home yet. There's a call of duty where He takes us to make a difference in the world around us. We are called to be a light to the world and out-shine the darkness. This doesn't happen through fear and condemnation; we are called to love one another.

The terrorists are not our enemies; they have been deceived. Don't get me wrong here: There is no justification for the acts we witness daily in the news of persecution and pure evil. I hate the acts of violence, yet I'm challenged to pray for the deceived who have responded to a broken world and found acceptance against God.

Making a difference

There is a battle going on in the heavenly realms that leaves consequences on earth. The Apostle Paul writes in his letter to the Ephesians, "For our struggle is not against flesh and blood, but against the rulers, against the authorities, against the powers of this dark world and against the spiritual forces in the heavenly realms" (Ephesians 6:12). We've got to choose sides and take action to make a difference.

I recently saw some statistics from a study done a few years ago and would expect the numbers to be even more disturbing today. Where are the Christian men? Christianity in America has been declining for a couple generations. We have more divorce, more kids with fatherless homes, increased suicides, depression and chemical dependencies. I think it's safe to say the enemy is taking territory at home and abroad.

I don't know if you like sports, but there are a lot of metaphors that can be used to illustrate the call to action required of men in the church. If you are on the team, great, we need you. The bride of Christ is adrift in a sea of deception that requires rescue. If we have a faith walk; a lot of us are lukewarm at best, and have settled into complacency and moral tolerance. Others are ambivalent and have been deceived into thinking it doesn't matter.

Seek God's will and listen for His voice, then follow His lead to go and make a difference in the world around you. Take a step toward action. If you're on the team, take off the practice jersey and get on the field. This isn't a scrimmage. If you are on the bench, get up and get on the field. The game isn't football; there's no penalty for having too many people on the field. It's more like Capture the Flag. We need to be strategic to be effective and that requires teamwork and fellowship.

There are tons of opportunities to get involved at your local church and ministry partners. Join a small group or get involved in a discipleship program like Be Resolute (beresolute.org). There are free online tools for discipleship like Operation Timothy available through (CBMC.com). Get out of your comfort zone for Christ's sake. He wasn't comfortable for you on the cross.

What are you waiting for? Someday never comes, it's always on the horizon of tomorrow. Tomorrow might be too late.

THE ENEMY

> "For the enemy has pursued me, crushing
> me to the ground,
> making me live in darkness
> like those long dead"
> (Psalm 143:3).

The contemporary church doesn't preach fire and brimstone from the pulpit like they did in days of old. Since the fall in Eden, there has been a struggle of good and evil, light and dark, righteousness and evil. We are the prize and our enemy is the devil. As a kid, I remember trying to use an excuse, *The devil made me do it,* a line made popular by comedian Flip Wilson.

The Flip Wilson show aired on Saturday nights in the early 1970s, and I would ask to stay up and watch it. Wilson would occasionally play a character named Geraldine. Geraldine would do something seemingly wrong and say, "The devil made me do it." In one episode, Geraldine blames the devil for buying a third dress in a week. In her defense, the devil lured her into the store; looking was free, and the store didn't charge anything to try the dress on. Then the devil pulled a gun and made her buy the dress.

My dad would get upset when I pressed the boundaries as a young boy and was caught making a mistake and tried to blame it on the devil. We may not say, "The devil made me do it," but we make excuses to justify, minimize and rationalize our behavior, which make moral compromise acceptable and tolerable. We don't have to look very far to see how things have changed in just a few short years.

Technology has given the enemy access to our daily routines and preferences, but we have been given everything we need to stand against temptation. The Apostle Paul wrote to the church in Corinth about overcoming temptation. "No temptation has overtaken you except what is common to mankind. And God is faithful; He will not let you be tempted beyond what you can bear. But when you are tempted, He will also provide you a way out so that you can endure it" (1 Corinthians 10:13).

Jesus was tempted by Satan, and we can learn from His account as written in the gospels of Matthew and Luke. They wrote to different audiences, yet their account is the basically the same. Today we can infer the lesson holds true for believers and non-believers alike. There's value in recognizing the two accounts are virtually identical in their telling of Christ's temptation.

Matthew 4:

> Then Jesus was led by the Spirit into the wilderness to be tempted by the devil. After fasting forty days and forty nights, he was hungry. The tempter came to him and said, "If you are the Son of God, tell these stones to become bread." Jesus answered, "It is written: 'Man shall not live on bread alone, but on every word that comes from the mouth of God.
>
> Then the devil took him to the holy city and had him stand on the highest point of the temple. "If you are the Son of God," he said, "throw yourself down. For it is written:
>
> "'He will command his angels concerning you,
> and they will lift you up in their hands,
> so that you will not strike your foot against a stone.
>
> Jesus answered him, "It is also written: 'Do not put the Lord your God to the test. Again, the devil took him to a very high mountain and showed him all the kingdoms of the world and their splendor. "All this I will give you," he said, "if you will bow down and worship me."
>
> Jesus said to him, "Away from me, Satan! For it is written: 'Worship the Lord your God, and serve him only. Then the devil left him, and angels came and attended him.

Luke 4:

Jesus, full of the Holy Spirit, left the Jordan and was led by the Spirit into the wilderness, where for forty days he was tempted by the devil. He ate nothing during those days, and at the end of them he was hungry.

The devil said to him, "If you are the Son of God, tell this stone to become bread. Jesus answered, "It is written: 'Man shall not live on bread alone.

The devil led him up to a high place and showed him in an instant all the kingdoms of the world. And he said to him, "I will give you all their authority and splendor; it has been given to me, and I can give it to anyone I want to. If you worship me, it will all be yours."

Jesus answered, "It is written: 'Worship the Lord your God and serve him only. The devil led him to Jerusalem and had him stand on the highest point of the temple. "If you are the Son of God," he said, "throw yourself down from here. For it is written:

"'He will command his angels concerning you to guard you carefully; they will lift you up in their hands, so that you will not strike your foot against a stone.

Jesus answered, "It is said: 'Do not put the Lord your God to the test.' When the devil had finished all this tempting, he left him until an opportune time."

These accounts are a content rich environment. I urge you to get into the Bible on your own, and pray for God to reveal His truth through the scriptures.

Further, I urge you to find fellowship in the body through Bible study and small groups to enhance your personal relationship with Christ. The larger body of believers is the bride of Christ regardless of denomination or name on the brick and mortar.

When we realize we are connected to something bigger than ourselves, we are equipped to make a difference in the world around us. "Then the God of peace will soon crush Satan under your feet. The grace of our Lord Jesus be with you" (Romans 16:20).

When we realize we are connected to something bigger than ourselves, we are equipped to make a difference in the world around us

God's Reality

- God – Seek Ye First
- Holy Spirit – Dwells in inner being
- Inner Spirit – Aligned with Holy Spirit
- Mind – Guided by inner spirit
- Body – Sacred vessel
- World – Light to the world
- Satan – Crushed at our feet

Figure 1

Figure one illustrates how we have inverted God's plan by exalting the enemy and live to survive Satan's illusion, oppressed by the world. God created us and wants to be first. We don't even realize we've marginalized God and have fallen for the enemy's lies. We are weighed down by the pressures of the performance-based world and have become distracted.

Our view is shaped by the world rather than allowing God's Spirit to lead us. We have a choice. Paul tells us in Romans 12:2: "Do not be conformed by the world, but be transformed by the renewal of the mind."

Jesus said, "Seek ye first the kingdom of God and His righteousness ..." (Matthew 6:33). God created us, and He wants to be first, not at the end of the day or the end of the week, but top of mind all the time. He wants to be in relationship with us. It's what we were created for: to glorify our creator and to be in fellowship with Him.

"Your enemy prowls around like a roaring lion looking for someone to devour"
(1 Peter 5:8)

CHANGE

I spent nearly 20 years in sales and marketing with one of the most innovative and diversified companies in the world. Commercial success comes in the form of products, services and processes that are recognized as solutions to a given problem, situation and satisfy a need or desire. The bottom line is that people buy, steal, take and get what they need or want most, regardless of the cost.

Marketing, promotion, advertising and media product placement are all means to position a product, service or process as a solution to change a want or desire into a need. People are often unaware they are targeted and provided a solution to a problem they didn't even know they had.

A successful salesperson is skilled at exposing needs, wants and desires through exploiting opportunities. There is need and opportunity met in even the most benign charitable transaction. I recall selling lemonade as kid or my daughters selling cookies for a school fundraiser. People—customers—had a need; they were thirsty or at least felt the desire to support a cause, and there was an opportunity right in front of them.

In a more commercial setting, exposing the need comes through a series of questions, discovery, fact finding and market research.

Any selling skills 101 class teaches the new sales person a simple technique of asking high gain questions: "If there were a way ... wouldn't you like to hear about it?" "The reason I ask is that our product 'XYZ' does exactly what you are looking for."

Bingo! The need is exposed, the solution is provided and the opportunity to close the sale is apparent. Then there is the whole matter of handling and overcoming any objections, which prolongs the sales cycle.

At some point the features, advantages and benefits exceed the cost of acquisition and a sale happens. The sales cycle has come to a close, and the prospect becomes a customer, the transaction has been completed and change has occurred. Business thrives on making change happen.

I began a second career in management consulting and found my niche in change management and process improvement. There are many ways to explain organizational change, process change, restructuring, corporate initiatives and objectives, but the one thing they all have in common is addressing the need for change.

The motivations driving the need for change are different: profitability, shareholder relations and safety are all good reasons, and the common denominator is that the status quo isn't good enough anymore. The process disciplines required for successful implementation of change management all have some key elements in common: identifying the problem, need or work to focus on, researching a strategic plan of action, putting the plan into action, learning from mistakes, making adjustments and continuous improvement.

As a consultant, I wasn't an expert in the mechanical details of designing a piece of equipment and engineering specifications or technical requirements for various performance requirements of the process. The consultant's expertise is focusing on process discipline, clarity of roles and responsibilities, and accountability for task function and execution.

Earlier we looked at the five Ws and the H: who, what, where, when, why and how. Using the illustration of process change in a consulting setting, who is the client; what is the scope of the project; where is the client site location; when is the timing of the implementation plan; why is the desired result of the investment into the solution; and how are the details of the consultant's implementation plan?

The critical question is the WHEN. When do you invest in change?

We've all heard the phrase, "If it ain't broke, don't fix it," which might be a good philosophy for little things that don't matter. You can wait to replace the batteries in the remote control for the television, but what if it's a broken headlight on your car? Sure you can get by for a short while with one headlight as a pa-diddle, but there is risk. You could be involved in an accident, and eventually you will get pulled over and at a minimum get a fix-it ticket or a warning from a police officer.

Let's say it's a flat tire; you are pretty much forced to change it right away.

When I was a child, my father was very practical, faithful and reliable. What I didn't know as a child was that when my dad was 10 years old, my grandfather left to serve in WWII. My dad was the youngest child, and my grandpa left him for the war while in his early 40s. He left his family and position as sr. pastor in his church to serve as a captain and became one of General Patton's chaplains.

The 134th Infantry landed on Normandy Beach, advanced through France claiming victory and critical position in the Battle of St. Lowe.

My grandparent's generation grew up through the Great Depression, survived two world wars and witnessed the industrial revolution firsthand. My grandfather's call to service was not questioned with any dissent; it was an honor and duty. None of this was understood by my dad as a young boy.

I can only imagine what those days were like for my dad; we never really talked about them. It was either too painful for my dad, or I was too young or too self-absorbed to ask any questions about a grandpa I never met. My grandfather survived the war but passed away from a heart condition shortly after returning from the war.

He wrote a few books about his war experience and opportunities to witness to young soldiers in battle: "He Is Able: Faith Overcomes Fear in a Foxhole," "The Sign That Saves" and "Overcoming Fear Through Faith." Thanks to the advances in technology and the Internet, I was able to find these books and learn of my grandfather's experiences.

As a result of my father's feelings of abandonment as a young boy, he grew up with different expectations for himself as a husband and father.

My dad didn't chase the bigger, better deal; he chose a career where he was home virtually every night. He could have tripled his salary with a position in business development with the company but chose to retire a business analyst. It was more important for him to be a husband, father and spiritual leader in our home than to be an executive. He worked very hard to provide for our modest middle class home in the suburbs of Minneapolis. Looking back, it's not that I grew up with everything I wanted, but I didn't go without anything I needed. I was blessed with parents who loved each other and to be raised in a loving, Christian home.

I grew up comparing what I had growing up to what other kids had: their toys, how they vacationed and where they vacationed. At an early age, I could tell the difference from our home and what I thought was a nice house. My friends might have had more square footage, newer cars and more stuff, but I never met their dads.

My home became the place my friends wanted to hang out, and my dad was always available after work. Mom and Dad somehow were able to get three busy boys to all the various sport practices, school events and church activities. As committed as we were being involved and busy, the summer family vacation was a sacred event.

Dad had three weeks of vacation plus recognized national holidays and an anniversary day off. The time off wasn't used to go golfing or fishing with his buddies. He was a family man and vacations were family vacations and family time. We typically took two weeks back-to-back in August after Little League baseball was finished and before school started. Since these were annual, big events, significant planning had to be put in place prior to the start of the vacation. The itinerary was mapped out and researched. We didn't need Travelocity, Priceline or travel agencies.

We never flew. Although cost was a factor, the opportunity for family time in the car, road-side museums, souvenir shops and captive family time was the real benefit. We didn't have smartphones, MP3 players, headsets, portable videos or any of the electronic and digital accessories we take for granted today. We had time for family discussions, reading books, playing travel games like *I Spy*, crossword puzzles and the like.

We would cover a lot of ground in those precious weeks as a young boy, and I was blessed to have those experiences to talk about when school resumed each fall. I learned it was less about the destination and more about the planning for wherever *there* was, the commitment of getting *there* and the family time of being *there*.

One year, we left Minnesota heading west through the Black Hills of South Dakota to Mount Rushmore, through Cody, Wyoming, to Yellow Stone, the Grand Tetons, Jackson Hole and back.

Another year we traveled east through Wisconsin Dells, Illinois, Indiana, West Virginia into the District of Columbia, Virginia Beach and back.

Every year we went someplace different. My dad loved the mountains so we typically headed west. Although the destination and stops along the way varied, one thing was always the same. The car was prepared for the trip.

To minimize the potential for mechanical failure and unexpected trouble on the road, the car was always taken to a mechanic for inspection and review of road worthiness. In all our years of road travel, we never broke down due to preventable mechanical issues. The car always started, ran well, and the brakes worked. The tires were always fit for travel, balanced and aligned. Only once did we experience a flat tire, and it was because some debris fell out of a pickup truck leaving a construction site.

Why change?

So what does this little trip down memory lane have to do with change? Well, most of us don't change until we have to. Most of us wait for a flat tire, treatment, jail or a heart attack to initiate our change process. Most of us wait until there is so much carnage from the train wreck that things are virtually irreparable and damaged beyond resolution. Most of us are provided with opportunities to change well before the recognized need to change. It's like somebody is trying to sell us something we don't know we need.

The sales cycle requires the benefits to outweigh the cost of acquisition. The change management consulting cycle similarly requires the process improvement, safety, quality, etc. to outweigh the expense of implementation, so that the return on investment satisfies the corporate director's expectations and shareholder dividend prediction.

The notion of God's grace is so foreign to us because the *Richest Cycle* is freely given. Jesus paid the price for our salvation. The return on His investment is our eternal life and all we have to do is opt in. There is no out-of-pocket cost, but change is required.

Remember the billboard: "Change Your Mind, Change Your Life." That's like trading in your old car for a new one. Our body, mind and spirit consist of self-centered inputs and attitudes made from our perceptions, ideas, opinions and beliefs. We need to trade them in for a new set of God-centered inputs, perceptions, ideas, opinions and beliefs.

"Do not be conformed to this world, but be transformed by the renewing of your mind, that you may prove what the will of God is, that which is good and acceptable and perfect" (Romans 12:2). God's design was for things to be good, acceptable and perfect. Now I'm not saying that once you become a Christian everything will be great; we still live in a broken world.

The criminal or addict may be incarcerated or in treatment for a period of time and be rehabilitated, but the reality is that the world hasn't changed. Our criminal justice system is saturated with repeat offenders, and there is a revolving door of addiction, treatment and relapse. Repeat offenders are common in our judicial system, and the best treatment centers function at less than a 50% long-term success rate, but God can make us new.

Our choice and the world

My perceptions, beliefs, attitudes, opinions and actions are results of my reaction to how I see the world and things happening in the world around me. So my perspective is based on how I perceive what is happening around me, and how what happens around me is applied to me and my place in what is happening.

"Perception is reality and reality is perception," said Charles Robert Simmons II. However, there is a difference between what is real (to us) and what is true. Stick with me through another automotive illustration.

When I turn the key, the motor starts.

This is real. I open the door and sit in the driver's seat. Everything around me is real. I can see the color of the interior, the dashboard dials and buttons. I can hear the noises of the street quiet when the door is closed, and the interior is muffled. I can smell the aroma of the pine scented air freshener hanging about the center console and almost taste the remains of a Happy Meal that wasn't discarded from the back seat after my daughter's soccer game last night.

The seat is in the familiar position with my expected proximity to the steering wheel, height from the floor and degree of recline. I check the mirrors, fasten my seatbelt and turn the key. The motor starts, and I can be on my way.

There is nothing more real about this experience. Based on my perceptions, beliefs, attitudes, opinions and actions, the car really starts.

The truth is there is much more going on than my myopic view from my perceptions, beliefs, attitudes, opinions and actions. In the blink of the eye when I turn the key, there is an electric pulse that causes a spark, which creates a controlled explosion in the combustion chamber in the starter that starts the motor running. The truth is that what was real to me and my experiences is not what started the car. The electrical and mechanical sequence of events that occurred subsequent to me turning the key started the car.

So then, we can look at the world of deception and illusion the evil one creates and recognize that we need to make a change in how we interact with the world around us. Most of us get comfortable with the status quo and don't change until we have to. We can look at change as risk, relative to frequency and effect.

We learn early not to touch a hot stove. The effect of touching a hot stove is immediate, and the consequence is painful; therefore learning takes place and behavioral change happens quickly. It doesn't take most of us too many times touching a hot stove to figure out it's not a good idea.

The other extreme is the story of a frog in boiling water. If you bring water to a boil and place a frog in the container, it will jump out immediately without much of an effect. However, if you place a frog in water of room temperature and slowly increase the heat, the frog will boil inside the pot without recognizing the conditions have changed to a fatal effect.

Addiction creeps up on people and destroys them in much the same way as a frog is boiled.

Let's establish a few things we can agree on: Good and evil exist; God and Satan exist as well, whether you believe it or not is your choice; the world is operating in a state of being separated from God's design by sin; and we can be reconciled by repenting of our sins and believing in Jesus as our Lord and Savior.

It's your choice.

NOW WHAT

"One of the greatest mistakes we make in our spiritual journey is circumventing the process of accomplishing our God-given dreams by trying to achieve them in a manner that violates God's character" ("Uprising 97").

Here is the call to action for believers. Jesus' message is a pretty straightforward four-step process:

1. "But ***Seek*** ye first the kingdom of God, and his righteousness; and all these things shall be added unto you" (Matthew 6:33).
2. God tells us to ***Listen***: "A voice came from the cloud, saying, 'This is my Son, whom I have chosen; listen to him'" (Luke 9:35). Jesus goes on to say, "Whoever hears my word and believes him who sent me has eternal life and will not be judged but has crossed over from death to life" (John 5:24).
3. He tells us to ***Follow***: "Whoever does not take up their cross and follow me is not worthy of me" (Matthew 10:38). Jesus said, "Whoever serves me must ***follow me***, and where I am, my servant also will be. My Father will honor the one who serves me" (John 12:26).
4. Finally, Jesus tells us to ***Go and Make***: "Go and make disciples of all nations, baptizing them in the name of the Father and of the Son and of the Holy Spirit (Matthew 28:19).

So in a nutshell, **Seek** Him first, **Listen** to Him, **Follow** Him and **Go and Make** disciples. This call to action sounds easy enough, but is difficult to sustain in a broken world full of Satan's deception and illusions.

The enemy is a skilled liar. We must remain steadfast with discipline and battle readiness "for our struggle is not against flesh and blood, but against the rulers, against the authorities, against the powers of this dark world and against the spiritual forces of evil in the heavenly realms" (Ephesians 6:12).

Simply put, as Christians we are in the heat of a spiritual battle with a tenacious enemy that seeks only to steal, kill and destroy.

As the body of Christ adapts to an increasingly intense environment of relentless spiritual conflict, we must strategically align our existing resources to develop, recruit and train for battle readiness. The enemy doesn't have any new and enlightened plots, schemes or ploys. His historically significant modus operandi has been to divide and conquer.

We see his schemes attempting to divide our people with politically volatile issues distracting us from our core values and principles. To be successful, we must unify our plan and commitment to established biblical principles and goals within leadership, transformation and sustainability.

"Seek ye first the kingdom of God and its righteousness; thy kingdom come, thy will be done on earth as it is in heaven."

Wholeness

We started this book with an illustration of skydiving, and the body's reaction to infuse adrenaline in the neurotransmitters as the body's response to the situational awareness of experiencing freefall. In much the same way, there is an infusion of God's spirit, the Holy Spirit, when one becomes part of the body of Christ.

This is not to establish an exhilarating expectation of an adrenaline rush type feeling of becoming a Christian. This experience does occur, but is not the same for everyone, nor does it determine the level of salvation in anyway.

The relationship with Christ is not an emotional response to a feeling that can sway with the wind, sound of music and personality of anyone on any given day. It is a matter of the heart and becomes manifest with an unconditional love from God.

We are designed to live in this way. We were created to be expressions of the goodness and wholeness of God. Good is to flow from our lives. Love is generative. It becomes an unlimited resource flowing from our hearts. We were created to know the full experience of love.

When God made mankind, it was very good. Apart from Him, there grows an all-consuming vacuum in the midst of our souls. In Him we are made complete and find that elusive state we describe as wholeness. ("Uprising," page 151). "The elusive state we describe as wholeness." I love the word choice here from Irwin McGregor in "Uprising" ... it points to the essence of the *awareness factor*.

There is something we must be clear on from the beginning regarding the *awareness factor*. The enemy will sneak in to minimize the effect as situational, coincidence, self-fulfilling prophesy and the like. After all, it's easy to find what you are looking for because you have to begin looking for it in the first place to find it. Herein the circular reasoning comes in to dissuade finding God's will. So in this case, we can refer back to Scripture: "They overcame (diversity, argument, objection) by the blood of the lamb and the truth of their testimony" (Revelation 12:11).

Allow me to share another story that simply cannot be explained away as coincidence. I found myself in discussion with some friends around the topic of current events in the Middle East. Our conversation was couched in leadership and America's role in international affairs. Throughout our discussion, I realized the environment we were in was very dry, I was experiencing cotton mouth, and my lips were dry.

As we wound down our conversation, I made a summary comment around something like, "I really need to have a better understanding of Israel's history, and I could use some ChapStick."

The next morning, leaving an event I was given a randomly prepared and selected gift bag as a modest thank you. As I began to explore the contents of the bag, I was eventually overwhelmed. The first item was a small booklet written by John Piper on spiritual leadership, which thematically supported the conversation from the previous evening.

The next item was a little more closely related to our specific topic of conversation, and my acknowledgement that I needed to learn more about Israel. It was a book entitled, "Rediscovering Ancient Israel," and then—you guessed it—ChapStick, not Carmex, Blistex or Vaseline lip balm, but ChapStick.

In that moment, I experienced a tangible encounter with our resurrected God. The odds of coincidence around the conversation, content, context and specificity to begin with would be astronomical to calculate—throw in the variability of random selection of individual gift bags and their specific content, compounded by the random selection of the bag itself is beyond any explanation other than miraculous.

But the significant part, what's really important and the crux of the story here is the context of the situation: The conversation was about seeking God's will in the Middle East, America's role and the importance of spiritual leadership; the ChapStick made it intimately personal and reinforced relationship.

The *awareness factor* can only be realized with hindsight. God is the only master of time and space and the only one who is capable of orchestrating events and revealing them with the end in mind before they occur. To recognize the epiphany moment, we need to be engaged in pursuit of His will. The word says, "Seek and ye shall find" introduced in Jeremiah and echoed throughout the gospels.

SEEK YE FIRST

"Seek ye first the kingdom of God and his righteousness ..." (Matthew 6:33).

Seek first, not second, not third; not at the end of the day; not Sunday; not when you are alone, in jail, over-dosed or desperate. "But seek ye first, the kingdom of God and His righteousness and all these things shall be given unto you."

The kingdom of God is the reality of what He designed for us to thrive in. A realm that is heaven on earth, which was in the garden at creation. A millennial realm when Jesus is back to reign in victory and what we hope for in heaven. The question is, "Do you trust Him?"

The Bible is a love letter, a heroic, romantic, epic story where love and life are equivocated. There is a hero and a villain in the story told from the beginning in the cosmos, played out in the sands of time through trial and errors, plagues and wars, bondage and freedom. We have a part to play in the story and the question is, "Do you trust Him?"

Either Jesus is who He said He was, or there is much adieux about nothing. I've played a little Black Jack in my day and spun the roulette wheel to bet on red or black, but are you willing to roll the dice on eternity?

This phrase from a song echoes in my head: "Love is a Battlefield."

> We are young, heartache to heartache we stand
> No promises, no demands love is a battlefield
> We are strong; no one can tell us we're wrong
> Searching our hearts for so long, both of us knowing
>
> Love is a battlefield.
> (Source: azlyrics.com, Pat Benatar – "Love Is a Battlefield")

I hear these lyrics in my head, and they take me back to the time in my life when I was a couple years out of college making a name for myself in corporate America. My whole life was in front of me. Then fast forward a couple of decades, and it hits me: Life is a battlefield.

Good and evil

There's been a struggle, a tug of war, back and forth battle between light and dark, right and wrong, good and evil. We see this from the beginning of the word in Genesis when light is introduced and takes over the darkness. Then in Genesis 3, sin pierces obedience and begins a domino effect, roller coaster ride of redemption, falls and building, in an epic battle for freedom.

What makes this difficult to put our mind around is that our experience is limited to a linear perspective. We live in a cause and effect world. The world asks us what we want to be when we are young and ties us to a performance metric at an early age. We find ourselves seeking approval from the world and striving for earthly status, oftentimes at the expense of those around us.

We can frame a battlefield in time and place, identify oppositional forces and from a historical context describe a war or specific battle. History is written for us to learn from. The author places the battle in context where lessons can be learned from those who came before us, so that we do not repeat mistakes.

Through context, we can explore political aspiration, strategy, economic value and motivations. However, when we add the spiritual dimension, things get a little more complicated pretty quickly.

The apostle Paul explains in his letter the church of Ephesus, "For our struggle is not against flesh and blood, but against the rulers, against the authorities, against the powers of this dark world and against the spiritual forces of evil in the heavenly realms" (Ephesians 6:12).

God's will

So when we seek knowledge of His will for us and courage to carry it out, we must be prepared for battle, not only in the here and now of what we can relate to from our experience, but in the spiritual realm as well.

Okay, I hope I didn't lose you. Stay with me here; let me try to walk through a real life example of seeking God's will in a critical decision regarding employment.

I found myself wrestling with God over the security I could find in the world of performance measurement realized with an annual performance appraisal, job title and income status. Annually I could compare my performance to a measurable economic value: how much money I made. If I worked harder and received a better performance appraisal, I could expect to earn more and improve my status in corporate America.

Now contrast that to seeking God's will and wrestling with obedience, faith and trust. Kingdom economics don't have a value stream based on a decimal point and commas. Jesus says, "Seek first the kingdom of God and His righteousness and all these things will be given to you" (Matthew 6:33). I refer to this as the *don't worry, be happy* message. Jesus is telling us to trust Him.

We've been created for so much more than simply to navigate our life's timeline to secure some treasures

We've been created for so much more than simply to navigate our life's timeline to secure some treasures. He tells us that the birds don't store up grain, yet they have food. The flowers don't labor, yet they are adorned in "all His splendor." Then He asks, "Can any one of you by worrying add a single hour to your life" (Matthew 6:27).

It all comes back to the question of trust. *Do you trust the creator?* Or are you deceived by the illusions of the world?

Go to God with your questions. The Bible says, "Seek first the kingdom." I dare you to ask God, *If you are real, show me?* Then be ready for Him to reveal Himself. If you call yourself a believer, I dare you to pray, *use me.* Then make yourself available for His use.

I hear stories too often from people who are frustrated and when I ask them if they have prayed about it, they just look at me like I'm crazy.

What's crazy to me is to allow something as powerful as prayer to go unutilized. God sent His son, Jesus, so that we could go to God the Father in prayer. He paid the price, atoned for our sin and tore the veil so that we could be forgiven and experience His presence. Yet a lot of us misuse or misunderstand prayer.

PRAYER
Matrix

	Low				High
High					
Low					

INTENSITY (vertical axis)

FREQUENCY (horizontal axis: Low — High)

The Prayer Matrix is a grid that illustrates our prayer life. The grid is laid out with two axis representing frequency, how often you pray and intensity and what the prayer is about. Somebody who never prays isn't represented on the grid.

- Low intensity, low frequency prayer is something like *"bless you"* when somebody sneezes.
- High intensity, low frequency prayer is the *God help me* car accident prayer.
- Low intensity, high frequency prayers are the daily prayers like, *Now I lay me down to sleep,* bedtime prayers or *God is great, God is good* meal-time prayers.
- High intensity, high frequency prayer represents intentional, intercessory prayer.

Intentional intercessory prayer is what Paul refers to in his letter to the church of Ephesus, "And pray in the Spirit on all occasions with all kinds of prayers and requests. With this in mind, be alert and always keep on praying for the Lord's people. Pray also for me, that whenever I speak, words may be given me so that I will fearlessly make known the mystery of the gospel, for which I am an ambassador in chains. Pray that I may declare it fearlessly, as I should" (Ephesians 6:18-20).

The quest to put God first and pursue His will for me came out of a place of brokenness. I failed to live up to the expectations I set for myself. The enemy tried to take me out. But in the quiet, God heard my prayer, *If you are real, show me.*

Then I listened.

LISTEN

"A voice came from the cloud, saying, 'This is my Son, whom I have chosen; listen to him'" (Luke 9:35).

The other day I was driving by a Little League ball field and saw something that brought me back to earlier years. I was drawn in to watch the group of young athletes as they ran down the field to a foul ball marker and turned to run back to the bench. The group consisted of about a dozen kids 10-12 years old.

Somebody had to be first and raced ahead of the others rounding the flag and began his return to the bench. Some of the young athletes turned short of the flag to return with the pack leader, while my attention was drawn to one young individual who wasn't in the lead and didn't turn short of the flag. He distinguished himself in what he did next.

He kept his pace in the pack and when he cleared the flag, he not only cleared the flag, but he turned around—a complete 360 degrees—and then resumed his pace to the bench. I laughed to myself as some of his teammates looked at him funny in response to his action, like, *Why did you turn a circle?* Then I overheard one of them say, "Coach didn't mean you had to completely turn around, you idiot." I thought to myself, *I've been accused of being too literal at times.*

Listening to God

I put myself in the shoes of a 10-year-old kid, trying not only to keep up with the other kids but trying so hard to do everything the coach said. In my mind's ear, I'm sure the kid correctly heard his coach yell something like, "Okay, you guys, we need to stay loose, run down to that flag, turn around and come back to the bench." So literal as his actions were, he did exactly what he heard the coach ask.

In the gospel of John, chapter 10, Jesus describes himself as the Good Shepherd: "I am the good shepherd." Later in the chapter He says, "My sheep listen to my voice."

So this really begs the question on how we hear God speak to us. Is it an audible, booming voice like thunder or a quiet whisper? Is it audible at all, or more like an inner dialogue?

The key is in the relationship, a personal relationship with God. "My sheep know me and they know my voice" (John 10:27). This comes with time in relationship.

You're not going to meet somebody for the first time and fully appreciate their sense of humor. Their dialect, tone and innuendo all build over time to develop a communication style that deepens the relationship. God created us in His image with one mouth and two ears, so we should listen twice as much as we talk.

So how do you hear God? Well, it begins with the relationship. Once you accept the truth that God is real, you have sinned and are forgiven through Jesus and have made a decision to allow Him to be Lord of your life, you've established a platform to build upon. We're able to do this through prayer, which is one way to communicate with God.

Like any communication, there is transmission and reception. We communicate through verbal and non-verbal, written and oral and other forms of expression as communication. It's easy for us to view prayer as a radio broadcast where we hope God is tuned in to our frequency and can hear our requests. It's easy for doubt to creep in and for us to feel like our prayers go unanswered. After all, He is busy, there are a lot of other prayers more significant than our own and somehow we feel ours are unworthy of His attention. Yet, we are in relationship with our creator.

If we make God small enough for us to comprehend, He's not big enough for what we need

We've got to quit trying to put the creator of the universe into a definition we understand: If we make God small enough for us to comprehend, He's not big enough for what we need. There are several examples in Scripture where God hears our prayers. He even sent an angel to tell Zechariah, "But the angel said to him: 'Do not be afraid, Zechariah; your prayer has been heard" (Luke 1:13).

That is where faith comes in.

Somehow we can accept in a fairytale kind of way that God knows the number of the stars in the sky, grains of sand on the beach and hairs on our head, yet He's too busy to hear our prayers. It comes down to trust. There are numerous references where people are pleading for God to hear our prayers, yet Jesus clearly says, "Therefore I tell you, whatever you ask for in prayer, believe that you have it and it will be yours" (Mark 11:24).

Our relationship is personal; communication is a two-way street. God hears our prayers, and we have to listen for His response. Now He may often (quite often in my experience) answer differently than we expect. When we want something now or seek clarity, His response could be, *Don't wait on me to do what I've gifted you for.*

Too often people put their head in the sand and wait on God and then get frustrated. Go back to the Prayer Matrix: Are you praying with frequency and intensity about what you are seeking?

His response could be that you need to wrestle with Him for discernment on what the wise thing to do is. He could just say, *No, be patient, you're not ready yet,* or (my favorite) *I'll show you*. Either way, understanding somebody comes with time, learning their style and appreciating each other's perspective.

Frequency and intensity

It's the same way with God. Jesus teaches through an illustration of the shepherd and his sheep. He is the *good shepherd*, and His sheep are His followers. The sheep know His voice, which means they have heard Him before. They have listened to Him and can tell the difference from the voice of truth or an impersonator.

You know what it's like when a friend calls you on the phone; you can tell it's him by his voice. Some people sound alike, and there are talented vocal impersonators, but they cannot speak for the real person.

Through context, tone, language and innuendo, you get to know people intimately, and our relationship with God is the same way. We learn through frequency and intensity; over time we build trust. It's important to learn to distinguish the voice of truth from the lies of the world.

There's a great song by Casting Crowns, "Voice of Truth," where the lyrics depict a couple of Bible stories we can relate to. There's the story of Peter and the faith it took to get out of the boat to walk on water; then the shepherd boy with a sling and a stone facing the giant. In both cases, they had voices telling them they couldn't do it. Peter succumbed to fear and lost his step on the water, and the boy believed the voice of truth and prevailed against the giant.

What voice do you listen to? The world tries to trap us in shame, guilt and un-forgiveness. I love the story behind the Matthew West song, "Hello My Name is Regret." He described in an interview that the inspiration for the song came from a letter he received from a fan. The fan introduced himself as Regret.

The lyrics say: "Hello my name is regret; Hello my name is defeat."

Then the chorus:

These are the voices, these are the lies
And I have believed them, for the very last time.
Hello, my name is child of the one true King.
I've been saved, I've been changed, and I have been set free.

Listening to the right voice

The final manuscript for this book had been sent to the editor, but there was a song I heard and I couldn't remember who sang it. The message was clear, but the lyrics were lost in my head. It was a bit of a running joke with friends who know I can chase squirrels and wrestle with the complications of how the mind remembers phone numbers from long ago, but sometimes forgets where the car keys are.

I woke up early and was compelled to find the song I couldn't remember. I scrolled through the radio station playlist and thought I might find it. I tried searching YouTube and Google. After all was said and done, I found "Name" by Nicole Nordeman. The funny thing is, this wasn't the song I was looking for.

Moments like this remind me that God has a sense of humor, and He has so much more in store for believers than we can imagine. It is because I have a personal relationship with God the Father, through Jesus Christ the Son, that the Holy Spirit can romance me through a spiritual dance.

The song I'd never heard from an artist I've never heard of said exactly what I couldn't make up. The song has a verse:

> Other voices you didn't know
> From the frey and the fringe they were all weighing in
> Now you can't remember who has your heart
> Well here's a start.

Chorus:

> You are still a promise, heartbeat of God.
> You may have forgotten but He has not.
> You are not your ashes, you are a flame.
> Do not ask the shadows the light of the world knows.

Refrain:

> You're a friend of God, God the son.
> Blameless and forgiven one.
> The slave no more, finally free.
> Sins and errors are now redeemed.
> Oh beautiful and broken heart.
> Is safe and sound in his arms.
> You were chosen; you were His.
> So remember this.

The song goes on: "You may have forgotten, but He has not. The reference to other voices, are enemy lies. We can listen to the shadows or the light of the world."

Lyrics like this remind us that we have competing voices in our heads. There's the voice of truth and the voice of lies. Which one are you going to listen to and believe?

FOLLOW

"Whoever does not take up their cross and follow me is not worthy of me" (Matthew 10:38).

Scripture says, "Do not be afraid" more than 80 times and "do not be anxious about anything" (Philippians 4:6). Then His presence fades into the background like a whisper, yet the feeling of being comforted lingers.

It's in these moments where I've been made aware and experienced His presence and that matters. I recognize that I'm part of something bigger. I've declared Jesus as Lord, and He calls me a child of God. I have decided to follow Jesus and am developing a relationship; I realize I'm in the family.

I remember running home from school on a Friday afternoon. It must have been Memorial Day weekend, because I was still in school. It looked like summer, but the air was cool and crisp; there was still a chill in the air, but the afternoon sun had taken over and things were warming up. We were going camping and I loved these kinds of weekends.

Who do you follow?

Camping was always a special time for our family. The weekend would include a drive up the North Shore of Lake Superior. God created us to be a part of something epic. There's a sense of adventure knit into our very being. The long drive allowed time to anticipate the impending adventure. We've lost something in our world of technology and dependence on continuous entertainment.

The North Shore provided a young boy a world of discovery. Sheer cliffs dropped over 100 feet to the cold clear waters of Lake Superior. The crystal clear water looked so inviting, yet it was treated like lava because if you slipped into it, surely you would die. Hypothermia and death by drowning were instantaneous in our "safety talks" on the drive. We knew to stay clear from the water.

Once the campsite was acquired and camp set up complete, we were free to begin exploring. Being the youngest of three boys, I always wanted to follow my brothers. There was a heightened sense of adventure when it was the three of us and since I was the youngest, I had to keep up. If I fell behind, surely I'd get lost, slip into lava water and die. Keep up or die was the summary scenario that played in my mind.

There was a certain freedom in following my brothers. They led the way; I watched and learned where not to step and to avoid slippery rocks. On certain paths, they would make the path clear, pulling away low hanging branches to avoid a slap in the face. One of them would caution, "Stay on the path ... there's poison ivy over there." "Okay, go slow here; it's slippery," and the occasional "grab my hand."

The security of having someone there to lead me while allowing me the freedom to walk in step or learn the hard way was comforting.

There were times my dad stepped in and said, "Follow me." "Stay close." "Hold my hand." "Whatever happens, DO NOT LET GO!" I knew in those situations there was danger lurking. I didn't even question my dad when I heard *that voice*. I knew I had to listen and pay attention or something bad could happen. Most of the time, it was okay for me to follow my brothers. Sometimes I had to stay back because I was younger. And sometimes I could go, but only if I followed my dad.

Jesus calls us to follow Him. In much the same way, the Holy Spirit leads us as we walk with our brothers. You can't choose your family, but you can choose the company you keep and who you follow. I was in pretty good company, most of the time. I found my own trouble when I strayed off the path.

We all have a choice in what we seek, who we listen to and what we follow. As a kid, I was prone to follow my brothers unless I heard my dad's voice call me in a different direction. As the relationship with God becomes intimately personal, the voice of God becomes more discernible, and you develop trust. As your trust builds, it's easier to discern His voice and to follow His lead.

My extra Bible and the beggar story illustrates what I'm trying to say here.

Being accountable

I was traveling and left my normal Bible in another location and took an extra Bible to Bible study. A few days later, I was reunited with my normal Bible. When I moved to put the extra Bible back on the shelf, I heard, was prompted by the Holy Spirit, God's quiet whisper, whatever you want to call it ... *Give it away to a street beggar.*

Mid-step on my way to the shelf, I stopped and kind of said to myself, "What? Like go out searching for somebody to just give the extra Bible to?" Then there was an internal dialogue with the voice of God. It went something like this:

No, put $20.00 in the Bible to cover his meal and feed him for life with My word.

Whose meal? I said to myself.

I'll put him before you; you'll know. Just put the $20.00 in the Bible and put the Bible in your car. Then wait. Don't go out of your way to make it happen. I'll put him before you.

The next two weeks I drove around with an extra Bible in the side pocket of my car. I'd been back and forth to the airport a couple times, and my normal routes weren't prone to beggars. I began to pray over this person the Bible was intended for.

One day, I found myself a few minutes early for an appointment and was led to underline Matthew 6:33, the cornerstone verse of Seek Ye First Ministries. Then I underlined Jeremiah 29:11: "'For I know the plans I have for you,' declares The Lord, 'plans to prosper you and not to harm you, plans to give you hope and a future.'"

I went into my meeting thinking I should underline the *Roman's Road,* the key versus to salvation.

After the meeting, I resumed my day and forgot about the extra Bible. Another couple of weeks went by with a couple more trips to the airport. Every time I opened the car door, I was reminded that I had an extra Bible with $20.00 in it for the first beggar I saw.

I continued to pray for this special beggar whom God had me set aside money for a meal and food for life … in a gift. I thought it would be really cool if the girls were with me when this special beggar appeared. They've never seen me give a Bible to a stranger, let alone give $20.00 to a beggar. That would prompt a special conversation about responding to hearing God's voice.

Then it happened. My daughter had an appointment, and I picked her up from school. Traffic was backed up on the interstate, so I made a move to navigate around the congested area and came to stop at a light on a surface street. I was in the right hand lane and there was a car to my left, turning left. Just beyond the car was a beggar on the corner. I saw him and all at the same time, the light turned green, the driver behind me honked his horn, and I eased through the intersection without a word to my daughter.

I dropped her off at the appointment and when I got back in the car, I saw the extra Bible. Immediately, my inner spirit was convicted that God had done exactly what He said He'd do. He put a special beggar in my path. The recipient of the extra Bible, $20.00 meal and food for life, who had been prayed over for weeks in advance was on the corner a few short blocks away. God even put my daughter in the car with me to experience the event, but I missed the opportunity.

At least I could still make delivery of the extra Bible and the gift of a meal and food for life. I worked my way back to the corner where the beggar had been, and he was gone. I looked around a bit bewildered and then saw the man across the street get on a bus. His sign was folded up, and he was gone. The story, weeks in the making had culminated in an epic fail on my part.

I could unpack the lessons learned from this epic fail for weeks of messages, and that's why the story is in this book. People want to know how to hear God, what their purpose in life is and how to really know if God is real. God sent His Son to die for us, so we don't have to die.

My dad called out to me on the North Shore cliffs above Lake Superior to follow him and keep me from harm's way. Jesus calls us to follow Him and sets an example in listening to God the Father's voice while responding with obedience. I heard God say, *Put $20.00 in the Bible and give it to the next beggar* I saw. I prepared the gift and prayed over it, yet failed to complete what was asked of me when the time came.

There's an element of time we're accountable for; we are infinite beings, in a finite body. God's going to get His way with or without you. It's your choice. "Many are called, few are chosen" (Matthew 22:14), which begs the question, Why are few chosen?

There's got to be a response to the call to be chosen. A friend of mine explains that it's like getting an appointment. There can be an appointment, but you have to accept the appointment. God will call and if you don't respond, He will call someone else.

In the story of the extra Bible, I'm left to believe that somebody else blessed the beggar. The good in it for me was to be able to write about it and hopefully shed some light on seeking God's will, listening to God's voice and following His lead with an obedient response.

The point is, we have a choice in whom to follow while we navigate our world tour. You only live once, right? The onus is on us; we are responsible for the path we walk.

Are you walking the path alone? Or are you following some brothers and sisters. Are you listening to your dad, or are you tuning him out because he's irrelevant and outdated?

Remember, danger lurks around the corner, there are slippery slopes, pitfalls and snares, pursuing what God has called us for.

GO AND MAKE

"Go and make disciples of all nations, baptizing them in the name of the Father and of the Son and of the Holy Spirit" (Matthew 28:19).

The Great Commission:

"Then Jesus came to them and said, 'All authority in heaven and on earth has been given to me. Therefore go and make disciples of all nations, baptizing them in the name of the Father and of the Son and of the Holy Spirit, and teaching them to obey everything I have commanded you. And surely I am with you always, to the very end of the age.'"

This side of heaven we can only imagine what it must have been like for the original disciples. Jesus was complete in Himself with the Father and the Holy Spirit, yet He had His inner circle. Peter and John argued over which one of them was His *best friend*, and James was His half brother.

Jesus was complete in Himself; we're not. He showed Himself as being fully God and fully human by depending on His three closest friends: His half brother James, Peter and John. The gospels of Matthew and Mark echo a verse that should humble us.

Speaking of man's salvation, "Jesus looked at them and said, 'With man this is impossible, but with God all things are possible'" (Matthew 19:26). And Mark, "Jesus looked at them and said, 'With man this is impossible, but not with God; all things are possible with God'" (Mark 10:27).

God didn't need man to save His Son, which would have been impossible. Jesus needed His friends to follow Him because he needed eyewitnesses of His death, burial and resurrection to fulfill the prophecies that prove He was who He said He was.

Think about it, these guys lived with Jesus for about three years during His ministry. No reasonable archeologist disputes the existence of Jesus of Nazareth. The historical written document preservation analysis of original texts from the period includes eyewitness accounts.

Man, alone, cannot save himself; man's salvation is dependent on God the Father, Jesus the Son and the Holy Spirit. Jesus could have saved Himself from death on the cross—He's God, all things are possible with God—yet He humbled Himself to endure the cross so that His inner circle and disciples could be eyewitnesses to His death, His Burial and His resurrection.

The gospel record of His initial resurrection appearances is pretty consistent, considering what must have been going on at the time. The Son of God, their Messiah was unjustly crucified and suffered the most brutal death imaginable. They all had to think they would be next and were afraid for their lives for three days.

Mark recounts that Jesus first appeared to two women (thanks for all the details Mark). Matthew gets a little more specific, naming the two women: Mary Magdalene and another Mary and later the disciples. Luke includes two travelers on the road to Emmaus, then the 11 remaining disciples in the upper room. John concurs with the others and includes some specific detail that when Jesus first appeared in the upper room, Thomas was missing. Thomas doubted the others' account, which is important for us to appreciate.

Jesus' closest friends lived with Him for almost three years, heard His teachings firsthand and saw Him perform miracles. They walked with Him, and believed He was who He said He was. Jesus told them what was going to happen, and it happened just as He said it would. He fulfilled their prophecies, and they needed to see Him with their own eyes, so that we could have their eyewitness testimony.

You can't make this up. The Jews wanted to stop the spread of the movement so bad, they had Him crucified. The Romans wanted to remove the threat of an uprising. The search for the body had to be one of the most thorough searches of all time. The authorities couldn't suppress the eyewitness testimony of those who reported seeing the risen King. They couldn't stop the movement then because people believed what they saw with their own eyes.

History as they knew it was redefined. As it stands today, the historical timeline changed at that defining moment in history, and Jesus Christ is the most pivotal person of all time. His ministry changed the world and continues to influence and define our existence and hope for the future today.

As believers, we are called to go and make disciples of all nations, baptizing them in the name of the Father and of the Son and of the Holy Spirit. Put simply, the church isn't growing because the bride of Christ is adrift in a sea of compromise, deceived by the illusion of tolerance. The body needs to raise up a generation of kingdom warriors and rescue swimmers.

I felt called to ministry and began to lay plans for an outreach and compassion effort that was simply built around Matthew 6:33: "Seek ye first the kingdom of God and His righteousness."

I used my personal testimony to encourage men of the church to do more than show up on Sunday. I saw myself as a lifeguard and wanted to pull guys out of dangerous waters before they drowned. I wanted to help men expand their comfort zone and connect with small groups and men's events to build fellowship, camaraderie and to encourage one another.

There's a wedding feast. We should be inviting all our friends, our neighbors, co-workers, even our enemies to meet the groom. There's going to be a reception and all are invited. Too many will ignore the invitation and put off their RSVP. When the banquet starts, the doors will be closed.

You Only Live Once

My daughter asked me, "Dad, do you know what YOLO means?"

"YOLO? What are you talking about? What's YOLO?" I'm thinking to myself: *Here we go again, now what? Is this another YouTube video I should know about?*

"It's text for You Only Live Once," she explained.

It shouldn't come as a surprise, but I didn't even realize that texting had become its own language.

"How Old School of me? There should be a text message dictionary for acronyms."

Nodding my head with a smile, holding up my index figure, trying to regain a modicum of cool, I said, "Wait, there should be an app with all the acronyms."

"Duh, dad, there already is one."

Strike two for dad.

"Well, there you go. So, what do YOLO for?" I asked.

She rolled her eyes and walked away. Over her shoulder I heard her say, "I was just curious if you knew what it meant, that's all."

So casually brought up as a question about a text acronym, I had just asked my daughter the ultimate question, "What do you only live once for?"

Think about it.

Her reply was equally if not more profound. "I was just curious if you knew what it meant, that's all."

Wow, aren't we all curious about the meaning of life? *A Purpose Driven Life* as Rick Warren puts it. YOLO. I never thought of it in terms of an acronym, but I used that phrase growing up through my teens and 20s, and it always had something to do with adventure. "Go for it, you only live once" or like Nike, "Just Do It."

I grew up as a church kid and pretty much stayed out of trouble. "YOLO" never had anything to do with drugs or anything. I guess I probably could have been labeled an adrenaline junky because growing up I/we (my brothers, friends and I) did a lot of dangerous things we could have easily been seriously injured or died doing. Another infamous motto of mine was, "Nothing to it, but to do it, so get to it, and do it to it."

Thank God that we survived that period of our lives with only a few broken bones collectively.

YOLO took on a bit of a personal twist as a teen-aged Christian. "You Only Live Once *and if you live it right, once is enough.* The implied message there is that if you lived a Christian life, you would have eternal life, which is entirely true whether you believe it or not. It is your choice. I just wish I lived out that simple motto so difficult to put into everyday practice in a broken world.

You can't read the newspaper, watch the news or even scan headlines from an Internet browser without some level of exposure to evidence of a broken world. There are corruptions and scandals locally and abroad from parents, school boards and churches to top government offices. There are scandals in our homes, neighborhoods, in the city and on the farms. Our world is perversely corrupted with drugs and alcohol addiction. Pornography, gambling, school shootings, gang violence and terrorism are everyday topics. This was not God's design.

God created you to live in freedom and within that freedom there is choice. What do you only live once for? Recognize that we are eternal beings in a finite body, and there is eternity. Whether you believe the statement to be true or not doesn't really matter. If I'm wrong, I spend my life fulfilled in relationship with others, putting them first, making a difference in the world and leaving a legacy on a tombstone. If you are wrong, you live as a parasite, only serving yourself and will have eternity to regret your choice. There's a path to salvation called the Romans Road.

Do you choose life or death?

Jesus said, "I am the way and the truth and the life. No one comes to the Father except through me" (John 14:6).

Salvation Prayer

If you choose life, make Jesus your Lord and Saviour

Pray this prayer:

God,

I know I need you. I come to you in Jesus' name, and I'm sorry. Please forgive me. Your word says, "If you confess with your mouth 'Jesus is Lord' and believe in your heart that God raised Him from the dead, you will be saved'" (Romans 10:9). I do confess with my mouth, and I do believe with my heart that Jesus is Lord, and I want Him to be the Savior of my life.

Thank You for saving me!

In Jesus' name I pray. Amen.

If you prayed this prayer for the first time, or rededicated your life to Christ - visit Seek Ye First Ministries **www.SeekYeFirstMinistries.com**, send an email to: **salvation@SYFministries.com** and share your testimony.

Welcome to the family!

Praise God!